Eyewitness
SHARK

Shark-tooth gauntlet,
Kiribati, western
Pacific Ocean

Pair of copepods, which
stick onto sharks' fins

Undulate ray

Angel shark

Model of a male
great white shark

Pair of baby dogfish

Shark-tooth
knuckle duster
from the
Hawaiian Islands
in the Pacific

Eyewitness
SHARK

Fossil
tooth of a
megalodon

Written by
MIRANDA MACQUITTY

Epaulette shark

Shark-shaped gold weight,
from Ghana, West Africa

Swell shark

Shark-tooth
necklace from
New Zealand

DK Publishing

Port
Jackson
shark

Pair of starry
smooth-hounds

DK

LONDON, NEW YORK,
MELBOURNE, MUNICH, and DELHI

Fossil of
Ptychodus
tooth

Project editor Marion Dent
Art editor Jill Plank
Senior editor Helen Parker
Senior art editor Julia Harris
Production Louise Barratt
Picture research Suzanne Williams
Special photography Frank Greenaway, Dave King
Editorial consultant Dr Geoffrey Waller
Model makers Graham High, Jeremy Hunt
Special thanks Sea Life Centres (UK)

Leopard shark

Long spear for
catching sharks,
Nicobar Islands, India

THIS EDITION
Editors Lorrie Mack, Sue Nicholson,
Victoria Heywood-Dunne, Marianne Petrou
Art editors Rebecca Johns, David Ball
Managing editors Andrew Macintyre, Camilla Hallinan
Managing art editors Jane Thomas, Martin Wilson
Production editors Siu Ho, Andy Hilliard
Production controllers Jenny Jacoby, Pip Tinsley
Picture research Jo Haddon, Sarah Smithies
DK picture library Rose Horridge,
Myriam Megharbi, Kate Sheppard
U.S. editorial Beth Hester, Beth Sutinis
U.S. design and DTP Dirk Kaufman and Milos Orlovic
U.S. production Chris Avgherinos

Shark rattle,
Samoa, South
Pacific

Ray-skin-
covered
scabbard used
by Ashanti
tribe, Ghana,
West Africa

This Eyewitness ® Guide has been conceived by
Dorling Kindersley Limited and Editions Gallimard

This edition published in the United States in 2004, 2008
by DK Publishing Inc., 375 Hudson Street, New York, New York 10014

Copyright © 1992, © 2004, © 2008 Dorling Kindersley Limited

08 09 10 11 12 10 9 8 7 6 5 4 3 2 1
ED627 – 01/08

A catalog record for this book is available from the Library of Congress.

ISBN 978-0-7566-3778-1 (Hardcover) 0-7566-0724-8 (Library Binding)

Color reproduction by Colourscan, Singapore
Printed and bound by Leo Paper Products Ltd., China

Discover more at
www.dk.com

Contents

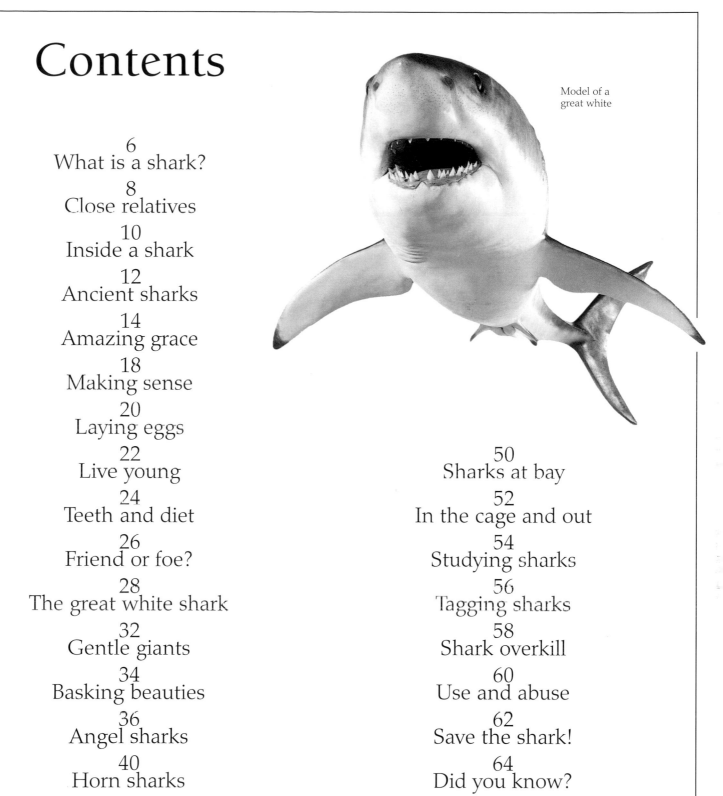

Model of a
great white

What is a shark?

MANY PEOPLE THINK of sharks as mean and menacing, with their pointed snouts, fearsome teeth, and staring eyes. Sharks are skillful predators, but only a few are a danger to people. The 450 or so species of shark range in size from a lantern shark, at about 8 in (20 cm) long, to the whale shark, at over 40 ft (12 m) long, but half the species are less than 3 ft (1 m) long. Not all sharks are as streamlined as this spinner shark. Angel sharks have flattened bodies, horn sharks are blunt-headed, while bamboo sharks are long and flexible. All sharks belong to one class of fish called Chondrichthyes, having skeletons made of gristlelike cartilage. Sharks live in the sea, though a few live in or swim into inland waters.

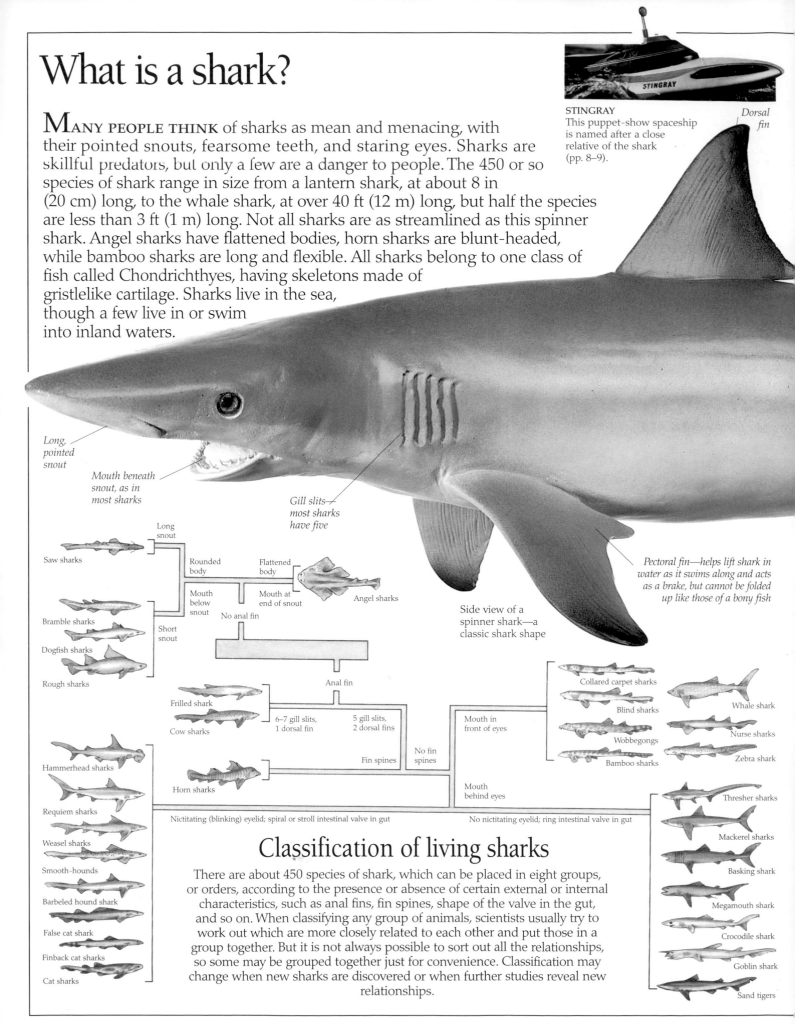

STINGRAY
This puppet-show spaceship is named after a close relative of the shark (pp. 8–9).

Dorsal fin

Long, pointed snout

Mouth beneath snout, as in most sharks

Gill slits—most sharks have five

Pectoral fin—helps lift shark in water as it swims along and acts as a brake, but cannot be folded up like those of a bony fish

Side view of a spinner shark—a classic shark shape

Saw sharks

Long snout

Rounded body

Flattened body

Mouth below snout

Mouth at end of snout

Angel sharks

Bramble sharks

Short snout

No anal fin

Dogfish sharks

Rough sharks

Anal fin

Frilled shark

Cow sharks

6–7 gill slits, 1 dorsal fin

5 gill slits, 2 dorsal fins

Mouth in front of eyes

Collared carpet sharks

Blind sharks

Whale shark

Wobbegongs

Nurse sharks

Bamboo sharks

Zebra shark

Fin spines

No fin spines

Hammerhead sharks

Horn sharks

Mouth behind eyes

Fin spines

Requiem sharks

Nictitating (blinking) eyelid; spiral or stroll intestinal valve in gut

No nictitating eyelid; ring intestinal valve in gut

Thresher sharks

Weasel sharks

Mackerel sharks

Smooth-hounds

Classification of living sharks

There are about 450 species of shark, which can be placed in eight groups, or orders, according to the presence or absence of certain external or internal characteristics, such as anal fins, fin spines, shape of the valve in the gut, and so on. When classifying any group of animals, scientists usually try to work out which are more closely related to each other and put those in a group together. But it is not always possible to sort out all the relationships, so some may be grouped together just for convenience. Classification may change when new sharks are discovered or when further studies reveal new relationships.

Barbeled hound shark

Basking shark

Megamouth shark

False cat shark

Crocodile shark

Finback cat sharks

Goblin shark

Cat sharks

Sand tigers

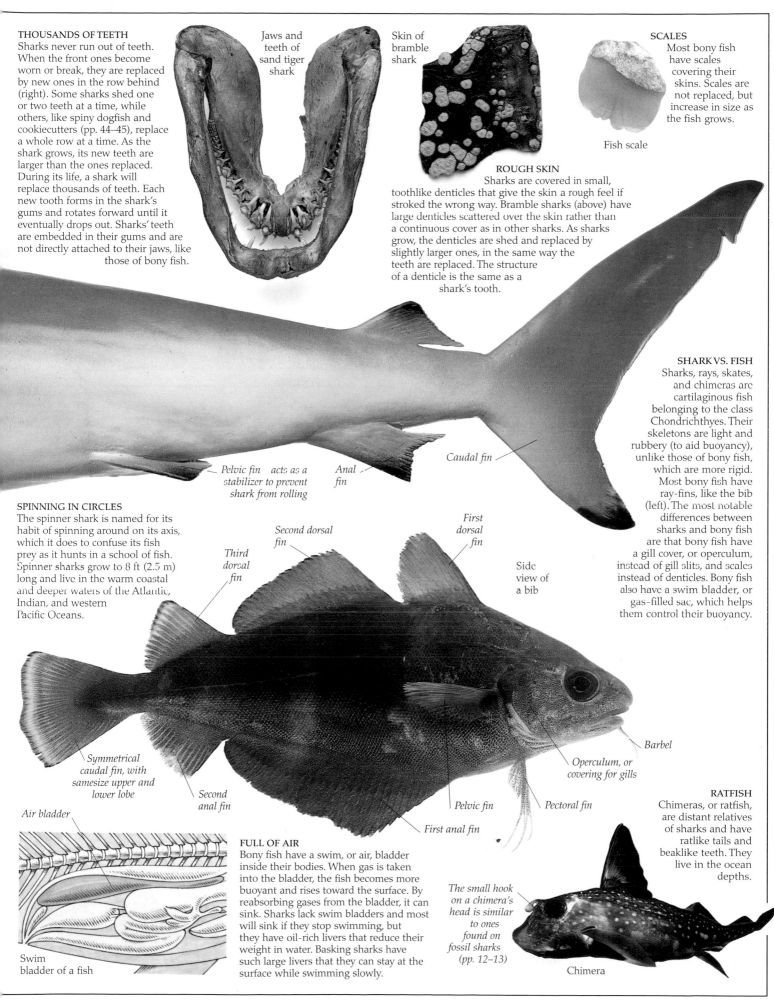

THOUSANDS OF TEETH
Sharks never run out of teeth. When the front ones become worn or break, they are replaced by new ones in the row behind (right). Some sharks shed one or two teeth at a time, while others, like spiny dogfish and cookiecutters (pp. 44–45), replace a whole row at a time. As the shark grows, its new teeth are larger than the ones replaced. During its life, a shark will replace thousands of teeth. Each new tooth forms in the shark's gums and rotates forward until it eventually drops out. Sharks' teeth are embedded in their gums and are not directly attached to their jaws, like those of bony fish.

Jaws and teeth of sand tiger shark

Skin of bramble shark

SCALES
Most bony fish have scales covering their skins. Scales are not replaced, but increase in size as the fish grows.

Fish scale

ROUGH SKIN
Sharks are covered in small, toothlike denticles that give the skin a rough feel if stroked the wrong way. Bramble sharks (above) have large denticles scattered over the skin rather than a continuous cover as in other sharks. As sharks grow, the denticles are shed and replaced by slightly larger ones, in the same way the teeth are replaced. The structure of a denticle is the same as a shark's tooth.

SHARK VS. FISH
Sharks, rays, skates, and chimeras are cartilaginous fish belonging to the class Chondrichthyes. Their skeletons are light and rubbery (to aid buoyancy), unlike those of bony fish, which are more rigid. Most bony fish have ray-fins, like the bib (left). The most notable differences between sharks and bony fish are that bony fish have a gill cover, or operculum, instead of gill slits, and scales instead of denticles. Bony fish also have a swim bladder, or gas-filled sac, which helps them control their buoyancy.

Pelvic fin acts as a stabilizer to prevent shark from rolling

Anal fin

Caudal fin

SPINNING IN CIRCLES
The spinner shark is named for its habit of spinning around on its axis, which it does to confuse its fish prey as it hunts in a school of fish. Spinner sharks grow to 8 ft (2.5 m) long and live in the warm coastal and deeper waters of the Atlantic, Indian, and western Pacific Oceans.

Third dorsal fin

Second dorsal fin

First dorsal fin

Side view of a bib

Symmetrical caudal fin, with samesize upper and lower lobe

Second anal fin

First anal fin

Pelvic fin

Operculum, or covering for gills

Pectoral fin

Barbel

Air bladder

Swim bladder of a fish

FULL OF AIR
Bony fish have a swim, or air, bladder inside their bodies. When gas is taken into the bladder, the fish becomes more buoyant and rises toward the surface. By reabsorbing gases from the bladder, it can sink. Sharks lack swim bladders and most will sink if they stop swimming, but they have oil-rich livers that reduce their weight in water. Basking sharks have such large livers that they can stay at the surface while swimming slowly.

The small hook on a chimera's head is similar to ones found on fossil sharks (pp. 12–13)

RATFISH
Chimeras, or ratfish, are distant relatives of sharks and have ratlike tails and beaklike teeth. They live in the ocean depths.

Chimera

7

Close relatives

A GRACEFUL MANTA RAY SWIMMING ALONG with slow beats of its huge wings looks nothing like a sleek reef shark. Yet rays and their cousins—skates, guitarfish, and sawfish—all belong to the same group as sharks, called elasmobranchs. Members of this group have cartilaginous skeletons, which are flexible like rubber, and gill slits, instead of the flaplike opercula, or gill covers, found in bony fish and chimeras (pp. 6–7). All rays have winglike pectoral fins joined to their heads, and gill slits on the undersides of their bodies. Most rays live on the seabed, where they feed on shellfish, worms, and fish.

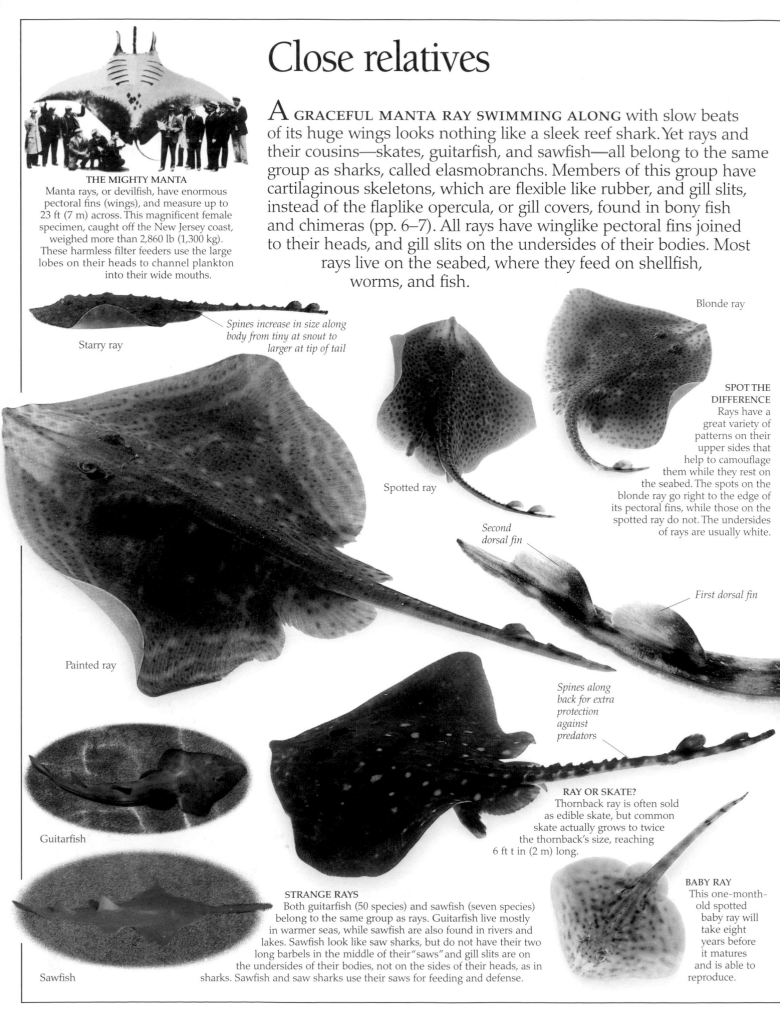

THE MIGHTY MANTA
Manta rays, or devilfish, have enormous pectoral fins (wings), and measure up to 23 ft (7 m) across. This magnificent female specimen, caught off the New Jersey coast, weighed more than 2,860 lb (1,300 kg). These harmless filter feeders use the large lobes on their heads to channel plankton into their wide mouths.

Starry ray

Spines increase in size along body from tiny at snout to larger at tip of tail

Blonde ray

Spotted ray

SPOT THE DIFFERENCE
Rays have a great variety of patterns on their upper sides that help to camouflage them while they rest on the seabed. The spots on the blonde ray go right to the edge of its pectoral fins, while those on the spotted ray do not. The undersides of rays are usually white.

Second dorsal fin

First dorsal fin

Painted ray

Spines along back for extra protection against predators

RAY OR SKATE?
Thornback ray is often sold as edible skate, but common skate actually grows to twice the thornback's size, reaching 6 ft t in (2 m) long.

Guitarfish

STRANGE RAYS
Both guitarfish (50 species) and sawfish (seven species) belong to the same group as rays. Guitarfish live mostly in warmer seas, while sawfish are also found in rivers and lakes. Sawfish look like saw sharks, but do not have their two long barbels in the middle of their "saws" and gill slits are on the undersides of their bodies, not on the sides of their heads, as in sharks. Sawfish and saw sharks use their saws for feeding and defense.

BABY RAY
This one-month-old spotted baby ray will take eight years before it matures and is able to reproduce.

Sawfish

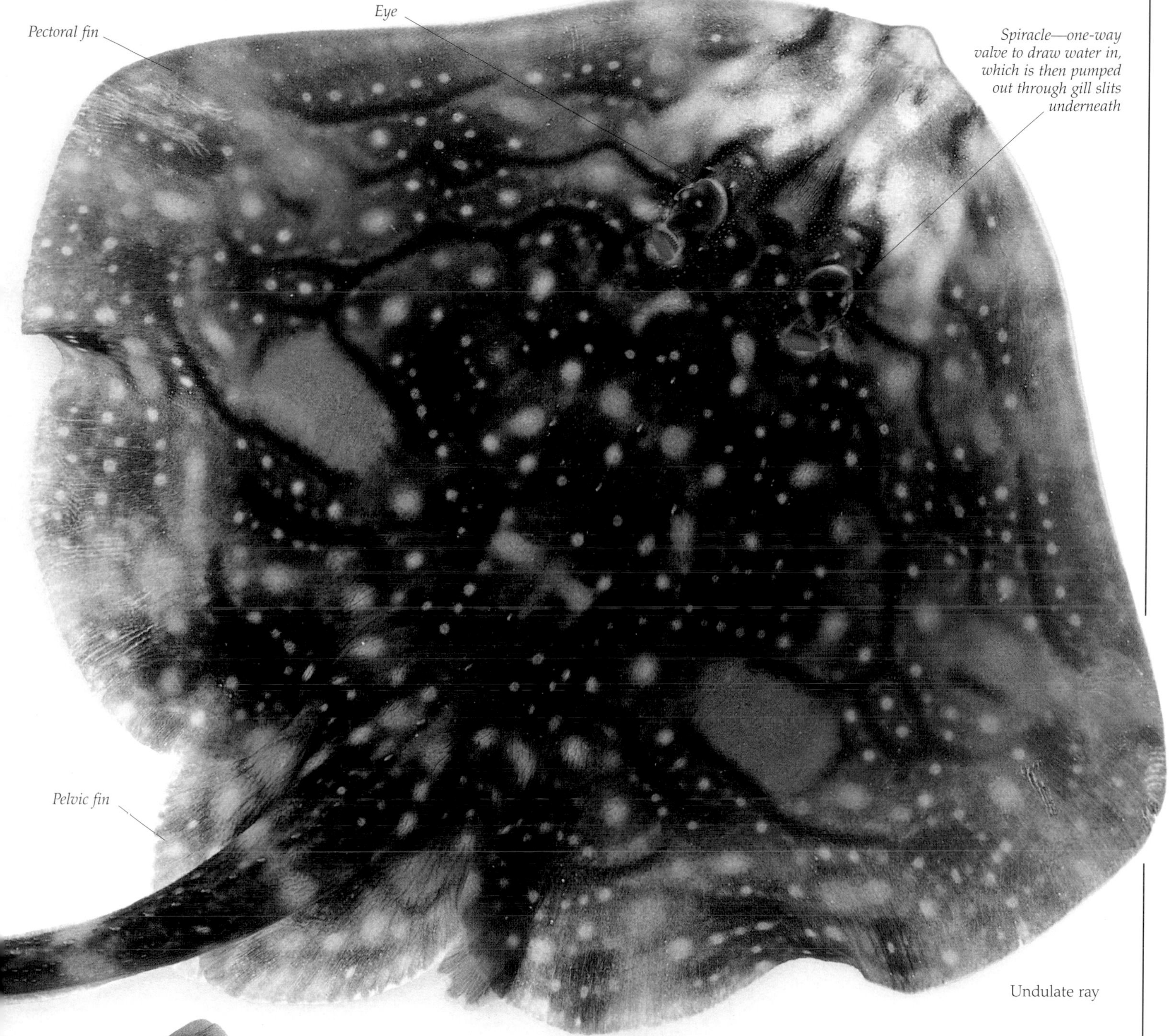

Pectoral fin

Eye

Spiracle—one-way
valve to draw water in,
which is then pumped
out through gill slits
underneath

Pelvic fin

Undulate ray

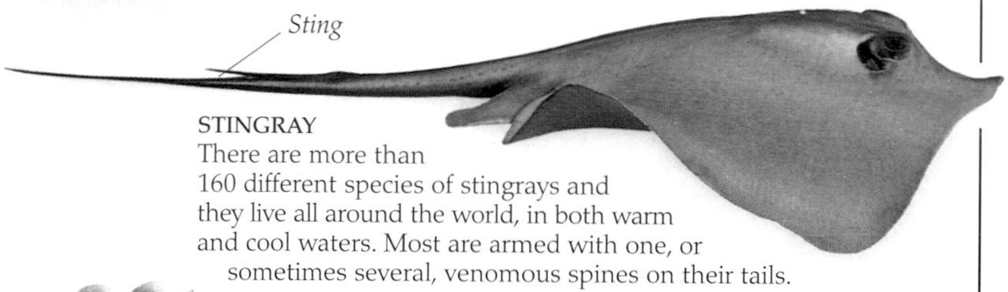

Sting

STINGRAY
There are more than
160 different species of stingrays and
they live all around the world, in both warm
and cool waters. Most are armed with one, or
sometimes several, venomous spines on their tails.

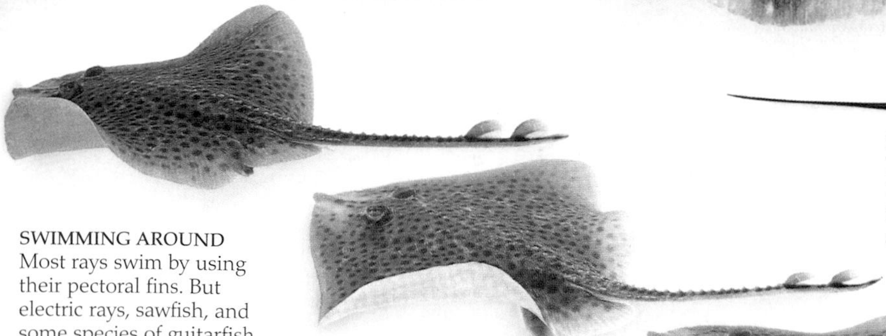

SWIMMING AROUND
Most rays swim by using
their pectoral fins. But
electric rays, sawfish, and
some species of guitarfish
swim in the same way as sharks do, by sculling
with their tails. This spotted ray's tail is too spindly to
provide much propulsion, so undulations, or waves, pass
down the length of the ray's pectoral fins from front to
back. As they swim along they appear to fly through the
water. The up-and-down motion of the pectoral fins, or
wings, is shown much better in species with enormous
wings, like the manta ray. These giant rays are even able to
leap clear out of the water, sometimes up to 5 ft (1.5 m).

Typical swimming
sequence of rays

Inside a shark

PACKAGED NEATLY INSIDE this spinner shark's body are all the organs that keep it alive. To breathe, sharks have gills that absorb oxygen from the water and release carbon dioxide back into it. These gases are transported to and from the gills by the blood. The heart pumps the blood around the body, delivering oxygen and nutrients, while taking away carbon dioxide and other wastes. To get energy for all their activities, including growth and repair, sharks need to eat. Food passes into the digestive system, which is like a large tube. From the mouth the food goes down the gullet into the stomach, where digestion begins, and then into the intestine where digested food is absorbed. Indigestible wastes collect in the rectum to be passed out of the body. Digested food is further processed in the large liver, which also increases the shark's buoyancy. Kidneys remove wastes from the blood and regulate blood concentration. Large muscles in the body wall keep the shark swimming, while the skeleton and skin provide support. The brain coordinates the shark's actions with signals or instructions passed back and forth along the spinal cord. Finally, sharks, like all animals, cannot live forever and must reproduce to carry on the species. Female sharks produce eggs from their ovaries and males sperm from their testes. When sperm meets egg, a new life begins.

DANGER BELOW
Sharks have been known to attack people coming down into water, as this Australian parachutist will soon discover.

Paired kidneys regulate waste products to keep concentration of body fluids just above that of sea water, or sharks will dehydrate

Segmented swimming muscles contract alternately, sending a wave motion from head to tail

Model of a female spinner shark, showing internal anatomy

Vent between claspers for disposing of body wastes

Clasper (male reproductive organ)

Male shark

Female shark (claspers absent)

Cloaca (opening for reproduction, and vent for waste disposal)

MALE OR FEMALE
All male sharks have a pair of claspers that are formed from the inner edge of their pelvic fins. During mating, one of the claspers is rotated forward and inserted into the female's body opening, or cloaca. Sperm is pumped down a groove in the clasper into the female, so fertilization of her eggs takes place inside her body.

Rectal gland (third kidney) passes excess salt out of the body through the vent

Scroll valve in intestine, or gut—other sharks have spiral or ring valves

Left lobe of large liver

Caudal fin

ALL IN THE TAIL
Sharks have a backbone, or vertebral column, which extends into the upper lobe of their tail, or caudal fin. This type of caudal fin is called a heterocercal tail, as opposed to those in most bony fish, where the upper lobe does not contain an extension of the vertebral column. Cartilaginous rods and dermal filaments help to strengthen the shark's tail.

Vertebral column

Cartilaginous rod

Dermal filament

BRAIN POWER

Some sharks have brains that are similar in weight to those of birds and mammals, when compared to their overall body weight. The nasal sac, or sensory part of the nose, is close to the front part of the brain.

Nasal sac

Forebrain

Midbrain

Hindbrain

Brain of a lemon shark

Ovary (eggs visible within its wall). When ripe, eggs pass into a tube for fertilization

Gill arch, with gill filaments, where respiration takes place

Cartilage support of gill arch, forming a hoop around the gullet

Jaw-opening muscle pulls jaws forward so teeth protrude

Nostril

Tongue is rigid, supported by a pad of cartilage

Jaw-closing muscle

Cartilage in floor of gullet

Aorta, with branchial arteries

Heart

Open gill slits (below)

Shut gill slits (below)

BLOOD CIRCULATION

Blood from the body collects in the first chamber of the shark's heart, then is pumped through the second and third, while the fourth prevents blood from flowing back into the heart. The aorta and branchial arteries circulate blood to the gills, where each branchial artery divides into tiny blood vessels in the gill filaments. As sea water passes over the gills, oxygen is picked up and carbon dioxide released.

Cartilage at base of pectoral fin

Cartilage of pectoral girdle supports pectoral fins and protects heart

Gall bladder

Pectoral fin

FOOD PROCESSOR

Food begins its digestion process in the shark's stomach, then passes into the intestine, where the multilayered scroll valve increases the area for absorbing digested food. A greeny-yellow fluid, stored in the gall bladder, is released into the gut, where it helps fats be absorbed. The shark's large liver also aids digestion, processing fats, carbohydrates, and proteins.

First dorsal fin

Stomach's descending limb

OPEN, SHUT

To breathe, water comes in through the shark's mouth, passes over the gills, and out the gill slits. A nurse shark pumps water across its gills, by closing its mouth and contracting the mouth and gullet walls. When the mouth opens, the gill slits shut, when the mouth closes, the gill slits open.

Second dorsal fin

Anal fin

Rear view of whole body of shark, showing gullet

Pelvic fin

Stomach's ascending limb

Spleen, producing red blood cells

Pancreas, producing enzymes to help digest food in gut

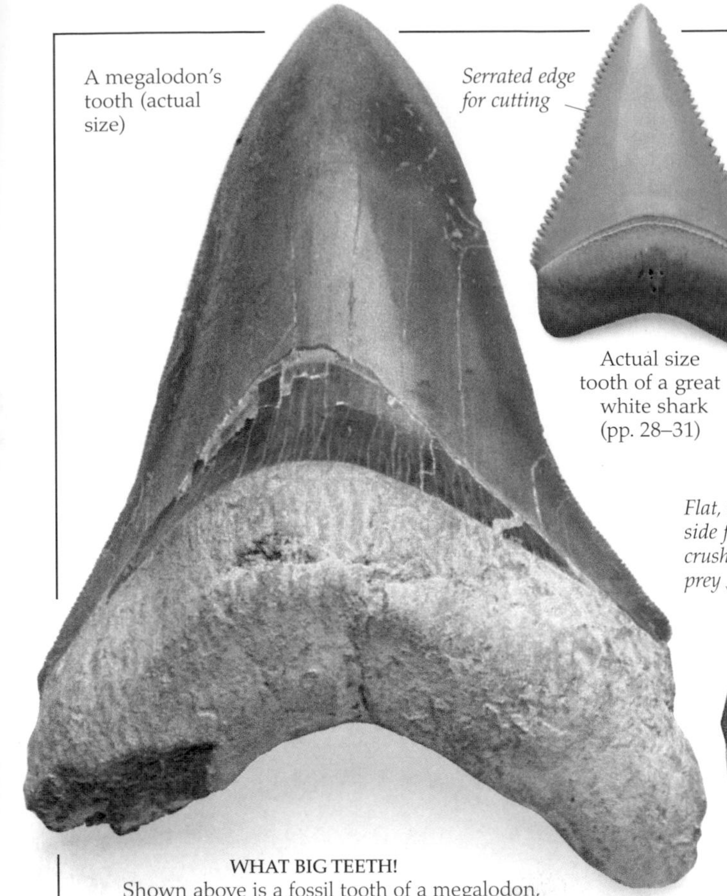

A megalodon's tooth (actual size)

Serrated edge for cutting

Actual size tooth of a great white shark (pp. 28–31)

Flat, ridged side for crushing prey

Tooth of *Ptychodus*

Ancient sharks

THE FIRST SHARKS appeared in the ancient seas 400 million years ago, about 200 million years before dinosaurs roamed the Earth. At that time there were no reptiles, birds, or mammals. The remains of some of these early sharks were fossilized when they fell to the bottom of the sea and became covered with layers of sand and other sediment. Hard parts, like spines and teeth, fossilized more easily than soft parts, which often rotted away. Sometimes all that is left are impressions of the sharks in rocks. Fossil shark teeth are common because these ancient sharks, like their living descendants, shed many teeth in a lifetime. Sharks' rubbery skeletons, made of cartilage, did not preserve as well as the hard skeletons of bony fish. Shark fossils are often discovered in rocks on land which, in prehistoric times, were under the sea. Scientists can tell how old fossils are from the age of the rocks in which they are found. The earliest groups of sharks became extinct, but the descendants of some groups that first appeared about 200 million years ago—like the bullheads (pp. 40–41), cat sharks, and cow sharks—are alive today.

WHAT BIG TEETH!
Shown above is a fossil tooth of a megalodon, or great tooth shark, compared to one from the great white shark. Megalodons reached about 52 ft (16 m) long and must have been formidable predators when they cruised the seas over two million years ago. A megalodon probably used its teeth for slashing deep into large prey, as great whites do today. The small, ridged tooth is from *Ptychodus* from 120 million years ago. These sharks probably ate shellfish, crushing them against the hard tooth ridges. They died out at the same time as the dinosaurs, about 65 million years ago.

JUST A JUVENILE
Looking much the same as its living relative—the lesser spotted dogfish (pp. 20–21)—this young shark died at least 65 million years ago. It is preserved in a piece of rock from the Lebanon in the Middle East.

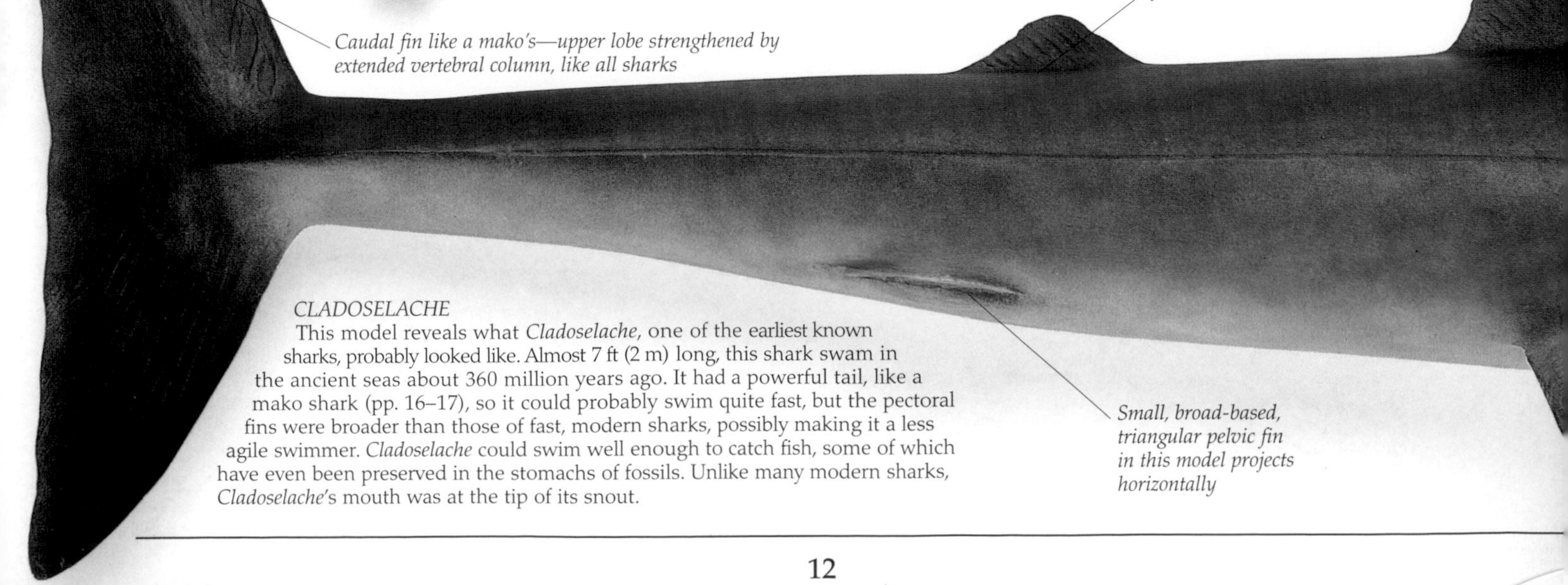

Second dorsal fin would have had a short spine in front

Relatively small dorsal fin, also had a spine in front

Caudal fin like a mako's—upper lobe strengthened by extended vertebral column, like all sharks

CLADOSELACHE
This model reveals what *Cladoselache*, one of the earliest known sharks, probably looked like. Almost 7 ft (2 m) long, this shark swam in the ancient seas about 360 million years ago. It had a powerful tail, like a mako shark (pp. 16–17), so it could probably swim quite fast, but the pectoral fins were broader than those of fast, modern sharks, possibly making it a less agile swimmer. *Cladoselache* could swim well enough to catch fish, some of which have even been preserved in the stomachs of fossils. Unlike many modern sharks, *Cladoselache*'s mouth was at the tip of its snout.

Small, broad-based, triangular pelvic fin in this model projects horizontally

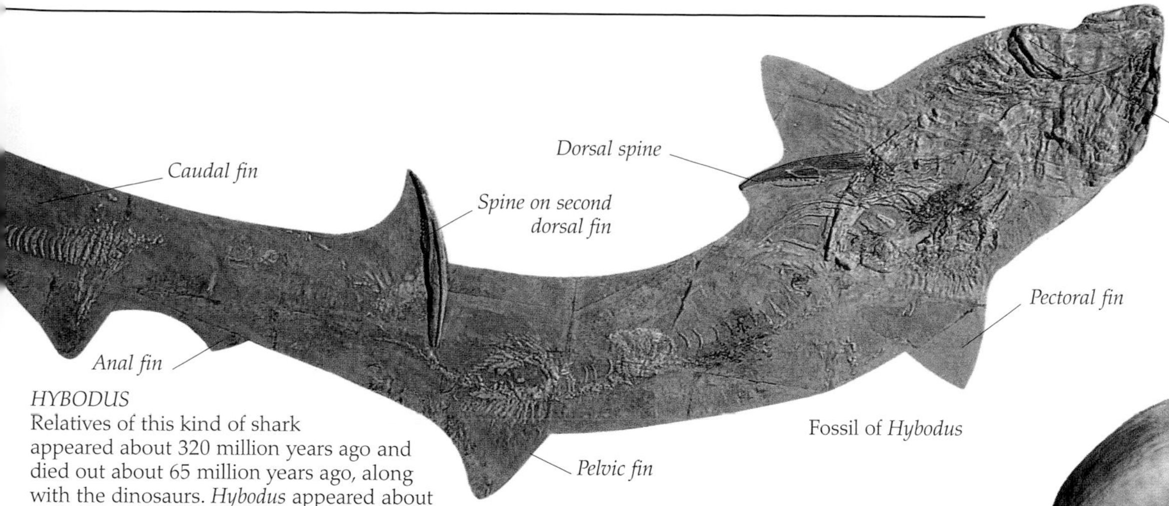

Caudal fin

Dorsal spine

Spine on second dorsal fin

Hook on head for holding female during mating

Pectoral fin

Anal fin

HYBODUS
Relatives of this kind of shark appeared about 320 million years ago and died out about 65 million years ago, along with the dinosaurs. *Hybodus* appeared about 165 million years ago and grew to about 8 ft (2.5 m) long. Males had claspers attached to their pelvic fins, as well as one or two hooks on their heads to hold onto females during mating. *Hybodus* also had an anal fin like some modern sharks.

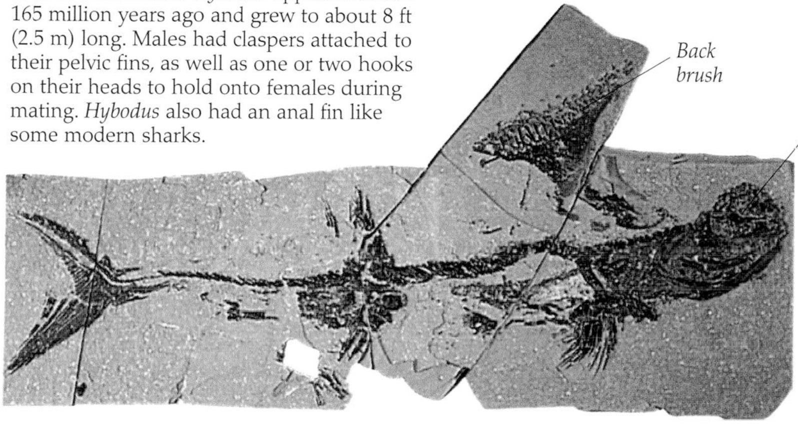

Fossil of *Hybodus*

Pelvic fin

Back brush

Head pad

BRUSH CUT
Stethacanthus, at 3 ft (1 m) long, was a strange looking shark with a big brush of denticles on its back and a pad of denticles on its head. The brush may have been used in courtship. Alternatively, the two sets of denticles, when opposing each other, could look like a big mouth and frighten off attackers. Whatever ate *Stethacanthus*, which lived over 300 million years ago, would have gotten a prickly mouthful.

GREAT WHITE JAWS
One of the largest sets of geat white jaws in the world is 22 ½ in (57.5 cm) wide.

FIN AND HEAD SPINES
Some ancient sharks had spines (left) in front of their dorsal fins, which may have protected them against large predators. Males of some early sharks had one or two hooks (right) on their heads for holding onto females while mating. Male chimeras still have hooks on their heads (pp. 6–7).

Fin spine

Head spine

Large, round eye

Victorian boy, 40 in (102 cm) tall

Triangular-shaped, broad-based pectoral fin

This model of *Cladoselache* has seven gill slits, but it is now known to have had only five

Mouth at end of snout, rather than on underside

GIANT JAWS OF A MEGALODON
A reconstruction of the jaws of a megalodon is shown above, with the jaws of the great white inside them to the same scale. There has been much speculation as to the size of a megalodon's jaws. Although an early estimate put them at 9 ft (2.7 m) across, more recent discoveries prove that a megalodon's jaws measured less than 6 ft (1.8 m) across, as shown in this reconstruction from the Smithsonian Institution in Washington, D.C. Megalodons are only known from their teeth and vertebrae. They lived from 2–20 million years ago. Scientists still debate if the megalodon was an ancient relative of the great white shark.

Amazing grace

SHARKS ARE GRACEFUL swimmers propelling themselves through the water by beating their tails from side to side. The pectoral fins are held out from the body and as water flows over them, lift is generated to keep the shark from sinking. Further lift is produced by the upper lobe of the tail, which tends to push the head down, so that the shark can swim on the level. Shark fins are not nearly as flexible as those of bony fish, but adjustments to the angle at which the fins are held control whether the shark goes up, down, left, or right. Pectoral fins are also used for braking. Some sharks that live on the seabed, such as horn sharks (pp. 40–41) and epaulette sharks, can use their pectoral fins to crawl along the bottom. Unlike bony fish, sharks cannot move their pectoral fins like paddles so are unable to swim backward or hover in the water. They also lack swim bladders, which act as buoyancy aids in bony fish. However, they do have oil-rich livers (pp. 10–11 that help reduce their weight in water.

"S" FOR SWIMMING
Sharks swim in a series of S-shaped curves and use a combination of fin angles to "steer" to the left or right.

TAIL END
Undulations, or "S"-shaped, waves pass down a shark's body as it moves forward (above). The tail bends more than the rest of the body, producing a forward thrust.

STARRY SMOOTH-HOUND
The denticles on a shark's skin line up with the direction of travel, helping to reduce drag (resistance to water). These denticles may trap a film of water, helping sharks move through it more easily.

CRUISING
With pectoral fins held straight out from its sides, the starry smooth-hound (right) keeps swimming at the same level. The two dorsal fins stop the shark from rolling and its tail gives a forward thrust.

One-year-old
leopard shark, 15 in
(38 cm) long

SEE HOW IT BENDS
Leopard sharks (above) have flexible
bodies, so they can turn around in
small spaces. Like their close relatives,
the smooth-hounds, leopard sharks
spend much of their time cruising close to
the bottom and also rest on the seabed.

IN FLIGHT
The large pectoral fins of the starry smooth-hound (left)
are similar to an airplane's wings because they provide lift to
keep the shark from sinking. When tilted, they can also act as brakes
like the flaps on the wings of an airplane that are raised on landing.
Submarines have horizontal fins, called hydrofoils, which lift them
upward like those of a shark. Just like hydrofoils, the leading (or front)
edge of a shark's pectoral fins is rounded and the trailing (or rear) edge
is thin, so that water flows over them more easily. The pointed snout and
tapered body are streamlined to give less resistance to water.

FULL STEAM AHEAD
A great white shark
(above) normally
cruises at about 2 mph
(3 km/h). Its bulky
body hardly moves at
all, while its tail beats
from side to side.
When closing in on
a kill, the great white
puts on an impressive
burst of speed of up
to 15 mph (25 km/h).

ON THE TURN
Great whites can bend
their bodies but are not
nearly as flexible as
smaller sharks. They
have to surprise their
prey rather than out-
maneuvering them.

15

Continued on next page

Continued from previous page

Tails and more tails

The shape of a shark's tail suits its lifestyle. Many sharks have tail fins where the upper lobe is larger than the lower, and as the tail swings from side to side, this lobe produces lift that tends to push the head down. This is compensated by lift from the pectoral fins, which stops the shark from sinking to the bottom. In fast sharks, like the mako and great white, these two lobes are almost equal in size. Lift may also come from the base of the tail which, in the mako, has small, horizontal keels. The extra height of these more symmetrical-shaped tails gives a more powerful thrust. Slow bottom-dwellers, like the nurse, have less powerful tails and their swimming motion is more eel-like, with obvious waves passing down to their tails.

BONNETHEAD'S TAIL
Bonnetheads are small hammerheads (pp. 42–43) that grow to about 5 ft (1.5 m) in length. Like all sharks, the tail's upper lobe contains an extension of the vertebral column and is usually larger than the lower lobe. The upper lobe is held at an angle so it is raised above the shark's midline (imagine a line drawn through the shark from the tip of its snout to the end of its body).

Tail of a bonnethead shark

THRESHER'S TAIL
The upper lobe of the tail (left) of a thresher shark is as long as its body. From 5–8 ft (1.5–2.5 m) in length, the tails of the three different types of thresher (pp. 58–59) are by far the longest of any shark. The tail of a thresher is used to stun its prey and also can inflict nasty injuries on anglers when the sharks are hauled on board.

Tail of a thresher shark

Tail view of a model of a great white shark (pp. 28–29)

Keel

GREAT WHITE'S TAIL
The upper and lower lobes of a great white's tail fin are almost equal in size. They lie high above, and low below, the shark's midline respectively. The keel helps the big shark to turn. The first dorsal fin is rigid and prevents the shark from rolling. Also a great white can jump out of the water.

ANGEL GETS GOING

To lift its huge body off the seabed, the angel shark beats its tail back and forth while tipping its large pectoral and pelvic fins for maximum lift. Once off the sea bed, angels propel themselves forward by sculling with their tails, but they do not undulate, or wave, their pectoral fins like rays.

MIDAIR MAKO

Makos (pp. 26–27) are probably the fastest sharks in the sea, reaching speeds estimated to be 20 mph (32 km/h) for a few moments. When caught on an angler's line, they leap clear of the surface in an effort to escape (above). Their tails are the same shape as another fast fish, the tuna, and like them they have keels along the base of their tails that may give them more maneuverability and perhaps provide some lift. They are active predators, pursuing mainly fish.

Lower lobe of angel shark's tail fin (pp. 36–37) is longer than upper lobe

SWELL SHARK'S TAIL

Smaller than nurse sharks, at just over 3 ft (1 m) long, swell sharks (right) are sluggish animals, spending the day resting on the seabed and at night swimming close to the bottom. Their tails are barely held above their midlines.

HORN SHARK'S TAIL

The lower lobe of the horn shark's tail (pp. 40–41) is more developed than the swell shark's. The tail of this 3-ft (1-m) long shark (right) is still held at a low angle to its midline and it is a slow swimmer.

TAIL OF A NURSE SHARK

Nurse sharks, at 10 ft (3 m) long, are rather slow swimmers and use their tails (right) for cruising close to the bottom.

Blue shark's nictitating eyelid

Sensory pores

Making sense

SHARKS HAVE THE SAME FIVE SENSES as people—they can see, hear, smell, taste, and touch. There is also a sixth sense that allows sharks to detect weak, electrical signals generated by their prey. This electro-sense may also help them to navigate on their journeys in the sea. This underwater world is quite different from our own. Light levels decrease with depth and colors fade to blues. Sound travels five times faster and farther. Odors are dissolved in water, not wafted in the air. Sharks can detect vibrations made by animals moving through the water, giving them the sense called "distant-touch." It is hard to find out exactly how a shark perceives its world, but studies on their behavior and how sense organs work give some idea about what it is like to be a shark.

Nostril

METAL DETECTOR
Sweeping a metal detector back and forth to find buried metal objects is like the way hammerheads (pp. 42–43) hunt for fish hiding in the sand.

GOING TO ITS HEAD
Like us, a shark's major sense organs are on its head. Seen on this blue shark are the eye, nostril, and sensory pores, which detect weak electric signals. The eye is partly covered by a third eyelid, called a nictitating (or blinking) eyelid, which protects the eye when the shark attacks its prey or nears unfamiliar objects. As the shark swims along, water flows through the nostril beneath the tip of the snout, bringing a constant stream of odors.

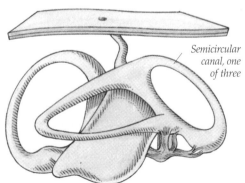

FEEDING FRENZY
When sharks are feeding on baits, they may become overexcited and snap wildly at their food. They may bite each other and even tear one another apart.

Semicircular canal, one of three

THE INNER EAR
Sharks do not have external ear flaps, but have ears inside their heads on each side of the brain case. Three semicircular canals placed at right angles to each other are like those found in the ears of all vertebrates. These canals help a shark work out which way it has turned in the water. Receptors in the inner ear, like those in the lateral line on the skin, pick up sounds traveling through the water. Each ear has a small duct that leads to a pore on the top of the shark's head.

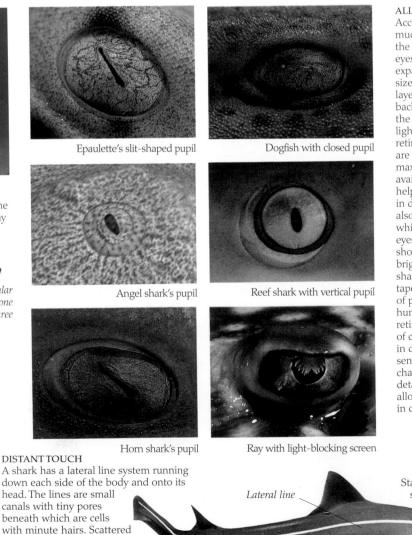

Epaulette's slit-shaped pupil

Dogfish with closed pupil

Angel shark's pupil

Reef shark with vertical pupil

Horn shark's pupil

Ray with light-blocking screen

ALL KINDS OF EYES
According to how much light there is, the iris in a shark's eyes contracts or expands to alter the size of the pupil. A layer of cells at the back of the eye, called the tapetum, reflects light back onto the retina, where images are focused, making maximum use of any available light. This helps sharks to see in dim light. Cats also have a tapetum, which is why their eyes reflect lights shone at them. On bright sunny days a shark can shield its tapetum with a layer of pigment. Like humans, a shark's retina has two types of cells—rods work in dim light and are sensitive to light changes; cones resolve details and probably allow sharks to see in color.

DISTANT TOUCH
A shark has a lateral line system running down each side of the body and onto its head. The lines are small canals with tiny pores beneath which are cells with minute hairs. Scattered over the body are similar hair cells called pit organs which, like the lateral lines, pick up vibrations.

Lateral line

Starry smooth-hound showing lateral line

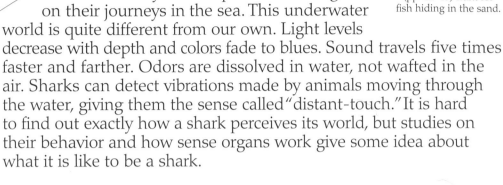

EYES ON STALKS

Hammerheads' eyes are on the end of their head projections, giving them a good view as they swing their heads back and forth. The nostrils are widely spaced on the front of the head, helping them detect where an odor is coming from. The head projections contain sensors that detect electrical signals from potential prey nearby.

Compass

Imaginary magnet

North-south axis

Earth's magnetic field

COMPASS SENSE

Some sharks migrate hundreds of miles and they seem to know where they are going, in what to us is a featureless ocean. Scientists think sharks have compass sense to guide them. In a real compass, a magnetic needle swings around to align itself to the Earth's magnetic field. The Earth's magnetic field (above) is created by its molten iron core, which acts like a giant magnet. Sharks seem able to swim in one direction by sensing changes in their own electric fields in relation to the Earth's magnetic field. Corrections have to be made for speed and direction of ocean currents, which may sweep the shark off course. Sharks may also be able to navigate by detecting magnetic patterns on the seabed.

DUCK-BILLED PLATYPUS

One of the few animals, aside from sharks, which has a sixth sense of being able to detect electric signals of its prey, is the duck-billed platypus from Australia. The platypus's electro-receptors are on the lefthand side of its bill. Platypuses live in streams where they hunt for insects and other small creatures on the bottom.

Nurse shark

Barbel

FEELERS AND TASTE BUMPS

The pair of feelers, or barbels, on the nurse shark's nose (right) means it can feel prey such as shrimp hiding in the sand. Many of the sharks that live on the seabed have barbels that they use to probe the sand for food. Barbels may also play a role in taste. Sharks have taste buds on bumps in their mouths and gullets (left). They spit out anything if they do not like the taste.

Nostril

NICE NOSE

Water is taken in through the epaulette's big nostrils and passed to a nasal sac where odors are smelt. Sharks can detect very weak odors—as little as one drop of fish extract diluted a thousand million times.

Snout of an epaulette shark

SPOTTY NOSE

The spots in front of the nostrils on this sand tiger's snout are sensory pores, called ampullae of Lorenzini. Full of jelly, the deep pores connect at their base to nerves. The pores detect the weak electric signals produced by their prey's muscles and bodily processes. Sometimes sharks are confused by electric signals given off by metal, so they will bite shark cages (pp. 52–53).

Laying eggs

FINDING A MATE, for some sharks, means a long swim because males and females live in different parts of the ocean. When they meet, the male chases the female, biting her to encourage her to mate. He inserts one of his claspers into her cloaca, or body opening. Sea water already drawn into a sac in the male's body is then squirted into a groove in his clasper (pp. 10–11) to flush sperm into her cloaca. In this way, the sperm fertilizes the female's eggs inside her body, unlike bony fish, where fertilization occurs outside the body with sperm and eggs being shed into the water. Fertilization may not happen immediately because some female sharks can store sperm until they are ready to reproduce. In most sharks, fertilized eggs develop in the female's uterus, or egg tubes, and she gives birth to baby sharks, called pups (pp. 22–23). In other sharks, the fertilized eggs are encased in a leathery shell and deposited by the female on the seabed. Once the eggs are laid, the female swims away, leaving them to develop and hatch on their own. These sharks are oviparous, which means their young hatch from an egg laid outside the mother—just like birds or bony fish.

MERMAIDS
Mermaids are mythical sea creatures with a woman's body and a fish's tail. Since ancient times, sailors have made up stories about mermaids. The empty egg cases of dogfish and rays that wash up on the seashore are called mermaids' purses.

CATCH ME IF YOU CAN
This male white tip reef shark is pursuing a female in the hope that she will mate with him. He may be attracted by her smell.

SPIRAL EGG
A horn shark wedges its spiral-shaped egg case into rocks to stop predators from eating it.

CAT'S EGG
The cat shark's egg case is firmly anchored onto anything growing on the seabed. Shark eggs are large and well protected and so stand a better chance of survival, compared to the masses of small eggs laid by bony fish.

LOVE BITES
When a male white tip reef shark gets close to a female (right), he bites her to arouse her interest in him. He will also grab her pectoral fin in his jaws to keep her close to him during mating. Very little is known of the mating habits of other large sharks.

THICK SKINS
Some female sharks, like this blue shark, have much thicker skins than males, so preventing serious injury during courtship. Most love bites are only skin deep and heal in a few weeks.

MATING SHARKS
People rarely see sharks mating in the wild, or even in aquariums. From a few observations, it seems that larger sharks mate side to side. White tip reef sharks (left) mate side to side and may pivot on their heads. The male of smaller sharks, such as dogfish (or cat sharks), is more flexible and wraps himself around the female when mating.

Tendril

Dogfish embryo

Yolk sac

Pair of dogfish egg cases

DOGFISH EGGS

Baby dogfish, or embryos, lie safely inside their egg cases. Every year lesser spotted female dogfish, or small spotted cat sharks, lay about 20 eggs in seaweed. At first the egg cases are soft, but soon they harden in the sea water. The tendrils at the corners of the egg capsules anchor them onto seaweed to prevent them from being swept away by currents. In the cool seas around the UK, embryos take about nine months to develop before they hatch. During this time each embryo gets its nourishment from its large yolk sac.

Pair of
10-day-old dogfish

Cream-colored underside

JUVENILE DOGFISH

These young dogfish are only 10 days' old. Although they are only 4 in (10 cm) long, they look like small versions of their parents. Shark pups are generally much larger and more developed than fry of bony fish. Soon after hatching, the young dogfish start to feed on small creatures like shrimp. It will be 10 years before they reach maturity and start to breed. When fully grown, dogfish are around 3 ft (1 m) long.

1 ONE-MONTH-OLD SWELL SHARK EMBRYO

Swell sharks live on the eastern side of the Pacific Ocean in shallow coastal waters. They are called swell sharks because when threatened they wedge themselves into a rocky crevice by gulping in mouthfuls of water. If taken out of the water, a swell shark can still swell up by taking in air. The female lays two eggs at a time, depositing them among clumps of seaweed. Each egg is protected by a leathery case. One month after it was laid, the fertilized egg has developed into a tiny embryo. A large egg sac is full of yolk that nourishes the growing embryo.

Coloring consists of light and dark brown bands, with dark spot on shark's top side

2 EMBRYO AT THREE MONTHS OF AGE

The embryo has grown much larger and it already has eyes and a tail. The yolk sac is connected to the embryo's belly by a cord, while oxygen in the surrounding sea water passes through the leathery egg case so that the embryo is able to breathe.

3 SEVEN-MONTH-OLD EMBRYO

By now the embryo looks much more like a baby shark. It has a complete set of fins and is able to wriggle about inside the egg case. The two rows of spines on the baby's back will help give it a grip on the egg case as it pushes its way out. The baby shark, or pup, will hatch as soon as it has used up the rest of the yolk sac.

Two-month-old swell shark pup

4 TWO-MONTH-OLD PUP

After 10 months, the young swell shark—at 6 in (15 cm) long—has hatched from the egg case. This is a most vulnerable moment in its young life, as there are many predators around. The juvenile's mottled color pattern makes it hard to see where it is hiding on the seabed. It can also wedge itself into its hiding place by swelling up.

Live young

THE MAJORITY OF SHARKS give birth to live young instead of laying eggs. Most are ovoviviparous, producing large yolky eggs that are kept inside the mother's uterus. The developing pup, or embryo, is fed by the yolk sac attached to its belly. When this is used up, the pup is fully developed and ready to be born. In some shark species, the first pups that develop eat eggs and also embryos in their mother's uterus. In sand tiger (pp. 24–25) and mako sharks, only one of the young cannibals survives in each side of the paired uteri, having eaten all its unborn brothers and sisters. A more complex pregnancy occurs in a few viviparous sharks, such as lemon (pp. 54–55), blue, and bull, as well as hammerhead (pp. 42–43) sharks, in which nourishment from the mother's blood passes through the placenta to the embryo via the umbilical cord. This is also how human babies develop, as well as other placental mammals, such as dogs and elephants.

MOTHER AND BABY
Human babies need to be looked after for many years, but shark pups are not so lucky. They must fend for themselves as soon as they are born.

1

HOW A LEMON SHARK IS BORN
(1) The tip of the pup's tail is just visible poking out of its mother's opening, or cloaca (pp. 10–11). Pregnant lemon sharks come into shallow coastal lagoons that are sheltered from the waves to give birth. Scientists studying sharks at Bimini in the Bahamas sometimes catch female sharks for their investigations. (2) Here, the female has begun to give birth. (3) The scientist is acting like a midwife and is helping the passage of the pup out of the mother's birth canal.

2

3

HAMMERHEAD PUPS
Hammerhead sharks give birth to live young that are little replicas of their parents. In one litter, up to 40 pups may be born, with their head projections bent back. In the uterus, each pup is connected to its mother by an umbilical cord.

BABY AFRICAN ELEPHANT
A baby elephant takes 22 months to develop inside its mother's womb, which is the longest gestation period of any mammal. This is not surprising since a baby elephant weighs more than 220 lb (100 kg) at birth. Some sharks have a nine-month gestation period, just like humans, although the spiny dogfish matches the elephant in taking 18 to 24 months to be born.

SPINY BABIES DO NOT HURT THEIR MOTHERS
Pushing a baby out of the birth canal is hard for any mother. At least the spines of hedgedog babies do not poke out through their skin until after they are born. The sharp spines on the dorsal fins of baby spiny dogfish have protective coverings.

BIGEYE THRESHER PUPS
As bigeye thresher pups develop inside the uterus, they feed on bundles of unfertilized eggs. The pups have long tails—just like their parents.

(4) The lemon shark pup, one of up to 17 pups, is still attached to its mother by the umbilical cord. She is nearly 10 ft (3 m) long, but her pups are only 24 in (60 cm) long. (5) The pup will rest for a while on the seabed, then swims away, breaking the umbilical cord. (6) Now the pup faces life on its own. It must seek the cover of mangrove roots and hide from predators, such as larger sharks and barracudas. For many years it will stay in a small nursery area in the shallows of the lagoon, near where it was born. Then it will make exploratory trips out of the lagoon to the coral reefs and will gradually spend more time further out to sea.

6

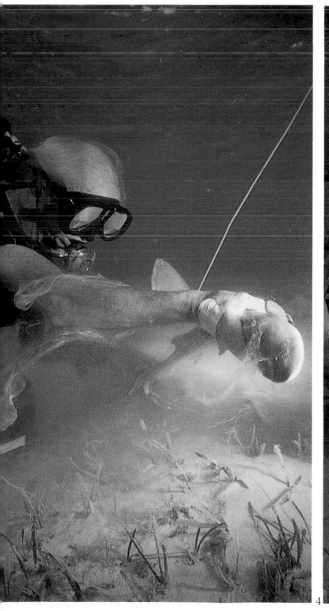

4

5

Teeth and diet

SHARKS CONTINUALLY lose their teeth. When the front ones wear out they are replaced by new ones growing in another row behind them. An individual shark can get through thousands of teeth in a lifetime. Animals, like elephants and seals, cannot replace their teeth and die when they wear out. As the shark grows, its new teeth are larger than the ones they replace. Sharks' teeth come in many shapes according to what kind of food they eat. Teeth, like small spikes, are used for gripping small prey. Serrated teeth are used for cutting. Long, curved teeth get hold of slippery fish. Blunt teeth crunch up shellfish. A few species of shark, like basking and whale sharks, have tiny teeth compared to their great size. They do not use their teeth to feed, but instead filter food out of the water. Some sharks produce different-shaped teeth as they grow older.

Tiny teeth of basking shark

Gill rakers

MOUTH WIDE OPEN
Basking sharks swim along with their mouths open to catch shrimp and other small creatures, called plankton, that drift in the sea. The food is trapped on rows of bristles called gill rakers as the water flows through the mouth and out through the gill slits. The gill rakers are shed each year during the winter months when there is little food around. A new set of rakers grows in the spring and then the basking sharks can start to feed again.

EPAULETTE EATING
Epaulette sharks live on coral reefs in the southwest Pacific Ocean around Australia and Papua New Guinea. They grow to about 3 ft (1m) long and can crawl along the bottom using their pectoral fins. These sharks search among the shallows and tidepools for small fish, crabs, shrimp, and other small creatures to eat.

SMILE PLEASE
Swell sharks (top right) from the eastern Pacific Ocean have big mouths for their 3-ft (1-m) length. Armed with rows of tiny teeth, these sharks eat bony fish that they ambush at night while the fish rest on the seabed. Only the Port Jackson's rows of small front teeth (bottom right) are visible when its mouth is open. At the back of its jaws are strong, flat teeth for crushing shelled prey.

Epaulette eating

Mouth of swell shark

CRUNCHY DIET
Port Jackson sharks have small, pointed front teeth to grasp their prey. The strong, flat back teeth can crunch through hard-shelled crabs, mussels (right), and sea urchins (below right).

Section through a Port Jackson's jaws

Mouth of Port Jackson

TIGER MOUTH

Tiger sharks cruise the warm waters of the world around islands and coasts of continents and often move inshore at night to feed.

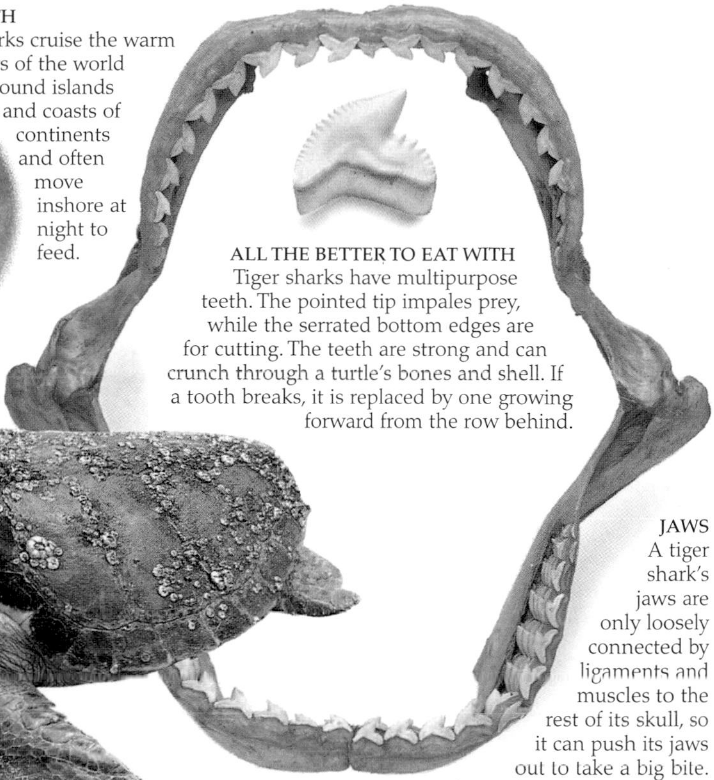

ALL THE BETTER TO EAT WITH

Tiger sharks have multipurpose teeth. The pointed tip impales prey, while the serrated bottom edges are for cutting. The teeth are strong and can crunch through a turtle's bones and shell. If a tooth breaks, it is replaced by one growing forward from the row behind.

DAILY MENU

Tiger sharks eat all kinds of food from squishy jellyfish to tough, shelled turtles. They are not put off by the jellyfish's stings or even venom from sea snakes which they also eat. Sea birds are not safe as tiger sharks will grab them from the surface of the sea. Carcasses of land animals, such as chickens, dogs, horses, and cows that have washed into the sea, are also eaten. Even tin cans, coal, and plastic bags have been found in their stomachs, and occasionally people are attacked.

Sea turtle

Jellyfish

JAWS

A tiger shark's jaws are only loosely connected by ligaments and muscles to the rest of its skull, so it can push its jaws out to take a big bite. When it feeds on large prey, it shakes its head back and forth to tear off chunks.

DISH OF THE DAY

Sand tigers eat a great variety of bony fish (left), as well as lobsters, small sharks, and rays.

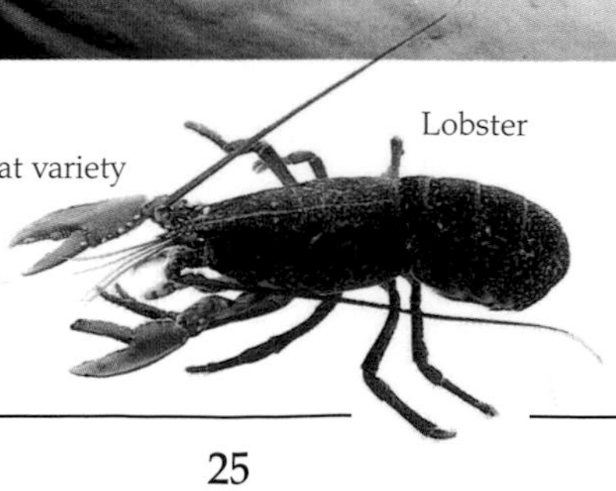

Goatfish

Lobster

RAGGED TOOTH SHARK

Sand tigers, called ragged tooth sharks in South Africa and gray nurse sharks in Australia, reach 10 ft (3 m) in length. Their long, curved teeth get progressively smaller from the middle to the sides of the jaw and are ideal for snaring fish or squid. They look fierce, but will only attack if provoked.

CLAWS

This ¾-in (19-mm) long copepod digs its sharp claws into a basking shark's skin. It feeds on skin secretions and blood. Basking sharks, infested by these and other parasites, become irritated and may even leap clear of the water to get rid of them.

Claw
Antenna
Head
Thoracic plate, or body section
Abdomen

BARNACLES ABOARD

This strange looking lump is a barnacle, related to the ones found on the seashore. In the sea, the larvae, or young, of this barnacle attach themselves to dorsal fins of spurdogs or dogfish. The root, or stalk, of this 1-in (26-mm) long barnacle has rootlets that absorb nutrients from the shark.

Soft shell
Root
Rootlet for absorbing food from shark

Female   Male

CLING-ONS

These small crustaceans, or copepods (½ in, 13 mm long), have adhesion pads to stick onto sharks' fins. They feed on skin secretions.

Friend or foe?

LIKE MOST ANIMALS, sharks have a variety of small friends and enemies that choose to live on or within them. Remoras benefit from sharks because they hitch a ride on them. They stick onto sharks using suckers on their heads, but they can also swim well on their own, as well as riding bow waves produced by a shark swimming though the water. Other kinds of fish, called pilot fish, also swim with sharks and ride their bow waves. Parasites harm sharks by feeding on their skin, blood, or even inside them. They may cause the shark discomfort, but parasites rarely kill the shark. Some parasites, like tapeworms, have complicated life cycles passing through several different animals before they can infect sharks.

CLEAN TEETH
Other animals have friends too. A bird cleans a crocodile's teeth and finds something tasty to eat.

STREAMERS

Copepods are clinging onto the dorsal fins of this mako shark (above) and have egg cases streaming out behind them. Each case contains a stack of disk-shaped eggs. When the eggs are released, they hatch into tiny young, or larvae. These larvae drift around in the sea, passing through several stages of development before attaching themselves to a passing shark.

STICKING TOGETHER

Shark suckers, or remoras (left), live in the world's tropical oceans. Each has a ridged sucker on the top of its head that it uses to attach itself to sharks and rays. While hitching a ride, remoras may do their hosts a favor by nibbling off skin parasites. They may also steal scraps when the shark has a meal and even feed on the placenta, or afterbirth, when a shark produces pups (above).

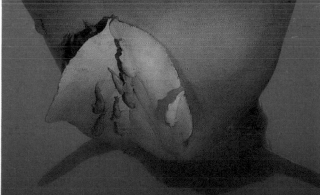

MOBILE HOME
Whale sharks (top) are so big that they provide living space for large numbers of remoras. Some remoras congregate around the mouth, even swimming inside the mouth cavity and gills, where they may feed on parasites, while others nestle around the cloaca on a female shark (above). Remoras get free transportation from their giant hosts, either by clinging on or riding the shark's bow wave.

WORMS AND MORE WORMS
Hundreds of 1-ft (30-cm) tapeworms may live in a shark's gut where, attached by spiny tentacles, they absorb food. Segments full of eggs from their tail ends are passed into the sea and the eggs hatch when eaten by a copepod. A young worm is passed on when a bony fish eats the copepod, and then a shark eats the fish.

Tentacle

Head

Body

Anchor which embeds in eye's surface

Arm

Head

Trunk

Egg sac, containing thousands of eggs

EYE SPY
This strange copepod hangs by its arms to a Greenland shark's eye. At 11¼ in (31 mm) long, the parasite makes it hard for a 20-ft (6-m) length shark to see. It feeds on the eye's surface tissues, but once there, it cannot let go.

PILOT FISH
Young golden trevally from the Pacific Ocean swim with larger fish, including sharks. Though they are called pilot fish, they do not guide sharks and other large fish to sources of food, but just like to school with larger fish. Also, they may gain protection because other fish do not like to be close to sharks. Pilot fish are much too agile to be eaten themselves.

NAVIGATING
A large ship is guided into harbor by pilot boats, but sharks navigate on their own (pp. 18–19).

The great white shark

A **POWERFUL PREDATOR**, the great white inspires fear. This awesome shark grows to over 20 ft (6 m) long and weighs more than 2.2 tons. It is the largest of the predatory sharks, capable of eating sea lions whole. The great white became famous in the *Jaws* movies, where it appeared as a blood-thirsty creature intent on killing people. Attacks (pp. 48–49) on people are rare, and possibly occur when a shark mistakes a person for its usual seal prey. Scientists are learning more about the great white, which is rare and on the decline in some oceans. Sharks are often studied around seal colonies. It is thought that great whites may interact with one another, slapping their tails against the water to ward each other off.

FRENCH LANDING
This old engraving of a great white landed on France's Mediterranean coast shows how a century ago people were also fascinated by sharks. Unless they were lucky enough to see sharks first hand, artists had to rely on descriptions to make their drawings since there were no photographs. There are several inaccuracies in this engraving—the artist has given the great white the tail of a thresher and gill covers, like bony fish, as well as gill slits.

Dorsal fin

Small second dorsal fin, compared to size of first dorsal fin

Pelvic fin

Long snout

Front view of model of a great white shark

Swimming keel

Upper and lower lobes of caudal fin are almost symmetrical (pp. 16–17)

Relatively small anal fin

Clasper

WARM BLOOD
Great whites and their relatives—the mako, thresher, and porbeagle—are all warm-blooded, which means that they are able to keep their body temperatures higher than the surrounding water. Only mammals, birds, and a few fast fish, like the tuna, are warm-blooded. These sharks have blood vessels in their muscles arranged in complex nets, so that the warm blood leaving the muscles passes heat to the cool blood coming from the gills (pp. 10–11). A high body temperature means that great whites have warm muscles that are able to act fast. This is important for a predator that has to make a high-speed dash to catch its prey. Being warm-blooded may also help the great white to digest its food more quickly. Scientists estimate that after a big feed a great white can last three months before needing another meal.

Pore marking position of ampullae of Lorenzini—sensory organs for detecting prey's electric field (pp. 18–19)

Long gill slit—one of five

Sharp, serrated teeth

WHITE DEATH
A great white's coloring makes it difficult to see in the water, so it is able to sneak up on its victims. When seen from below, this shark's white undersides blend in with a bright sky's reflection at the water's surface. This magnificent shark is sometimes called "white pointer," referring to its pointed snout, which makes it more streamlined. Great whites often have scratches and scars on their snouts that may be the result of their prey fighting back. They may also be bitten by larger members of their own kind that move in to take bait away from them.

Full-length side view of model of a male great white shark

Pectoral fin

TAKING THE BAIT
Scientists, filmmakers, and photographers use chum (a mixture of oil, blood, and horsemeat as well as tuna and mackerel) and baits to attract great whites. These are among the few sharks that stick their heads out of the water before and, sometimes, during attacks on prey. As the shark takes the bait, its eyes roll back in their sockets revealing the white surface of the eyeball. This protects the more vital front part of the eye from being scratched, which could happen if the shark was attacking live prey, such as a seal armed with claws and teeth.

TAGGING A GREAT WHITE
Dr. John McCosker, an American shark scientist, tags a great white off the Australian coast (top). Sonic tags have revealed that a great white can cruise at 2 mph (3 km/h), traveling about 120 miles (200 km) in three days (above).

Continued on next page

Distribution of the great white shark

BIG BITE
A great white's upper jaw protrudes forward and its snout is tipped upward (right), so it can grab a chunk of meat. This shark may have become accustomed to feeding from a rope because the shark's eyes face forward and are not rolled back as is normal when attacking live prey.

0 1,200 2,400 3,600 miles

What a great white eats

Great white sharks live in the cool to warm waters along the coasts of the Americas, north and south Africa, the Mediterranean, Japan, China, Korea, Australia, and New Zealand. They also swim across oceans and occur around some islands in the mid-Pacific and Atlantic Oceans. They are often seen near seal colonies, where they prey on both adults and young, but only a few sharks seem to hunt in any one area. When hunting a seal or a sea lion, a great white charges through the water, then attacks from below. Such is the force of the charge, the great white may even jump high into the air. Its victim may be released for a while before the shark returns to finish it off. The great white's diet changes as it grows up. Young sharks of about 7–10 ft (2–3 m) long eat mostly fish, while older sharks around 13 ft (4 m) long tackle larger prey such as seals and sea lions.

ON THE MENU
Great whites eat a variety of animals including bony fish, other sharks, some sea birds, marine mammals (such as seals and porpoises), and, occasionally, people! Penguins in South Africa are used for target practice, but are not usually eaten. Great whites are also scavengers and will eat whale carcasses and other dead animals.

Diver for dinner

Leopard sharks (above) are eaten by young great whites along the Pacific coast of North America

Bony fish, such as cabezon (above), are eaten by young great whites along the Pacific coast of North America

California sea lions (right) are eaten by adult great whites

TOP TIGER
Tigers and great whites are the top predators of land and sea, respectively. As adults, no other animals eat them, though they are killed by people. However, tigers, like great whites, sometimes eat people.

Scientists have found remains of jackass penguins, from South Africa, with bite marks made by great whites

Young elephant seals (above) are easy prey

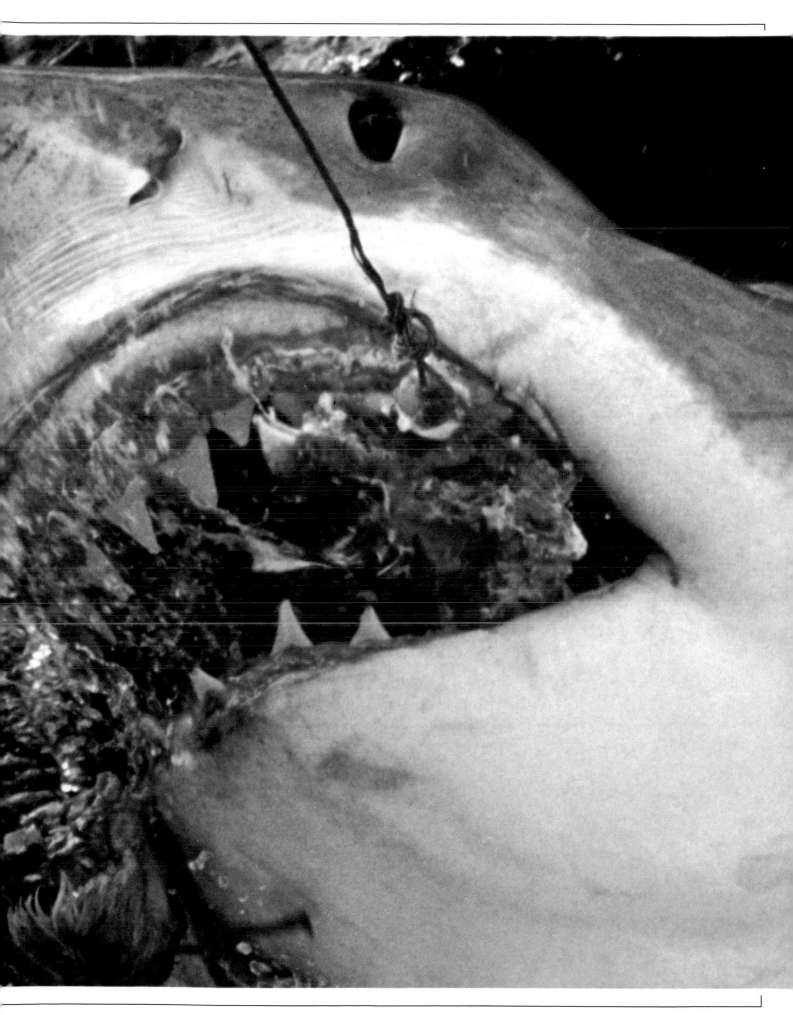

Gentle giants

HUMPBACK WHALES
Whale sharks are named after those other ocean giants—the whales—which are not fish but mammals.

WHALE SHARKS are the largest fish in the world, reaching at least 40 ft (12 m) long and weighing 14 tons, about as large as an adult gray whale. These docile sharks are harmless. The only danger they pose to snorkellers and scuba divers is to get knocked accidentally by the huge tail as it swings back and forth, or to be scraped by their rough skin. These giant fish can cruise at 2 mph (3 km/h), often near the surface—being so large they have been run into by ships. They live in warm tropical waters in places where there is a good supply of food to support their large bulk, and feed by filtering food out of the water. Whale sharks give birth to as many as 300 pups, hatched from eggs inside their bodies (pp. 20–23).

1,200 2,400 3,600 miles

AT THE DENTIST
People use their teeth to chew food. If their teeth are removed, they need to be replaced by false ones.

NOT MUCH OF A BITE
Whale sharks do not bite or chew food, so they do not need their teeth, which are no bigger than a match head.

Distribution of whale sharks

A GREAT GULP
Despite their great size, whale sharks feed on plankton (small animals that drift in the sea), small fish, and squid. Other large fish, such as basking sharks (pp. 34–35), manta rays (pp. 8–9), and baleen whales also feed by filtering food out of the water. Whale sharks scoop up water into their huge mouths and, as water passes over their gills and out through their gill slits, food is strained in filters attached to the gills. These filters are made up of a mesh of tissues supported by cartilaginous rods. Whale sharks occasionally eat larger fish such as mackerel and tuna, which are swallowed as they scoop up shoals of tiny fish. They can feed in a vertical position, even sticking their heads out of the water and sinking down to draw large fish into their mouths.

White-spotted bamboo sharks grow to about 37 in (95 cm long)

Anal fin

Brown-banded bamboo sharks grow to just over 3 ft (1 m) long

Nurse sharks grow to 10 ft (3 m) long

Barbel

Epaulette sharks grow to just over 3 ft (1 m) long

ONE BIG HAPPY FAMILY

Although they are much smaller, these four sharks (white-spotted and brown-banded bamboos, nurse, and epaulette) all belong to the same group as the whale shark. The main features they have in common are the presence of an anal fin and the position of their mouths well in front of their eyes. They also have two barbels on the tips of their snouts that help them find food. Unlike the whale shark, these much smaller sharks all live on the seabed.

Basking beauties

Cruising along with their huge mouths wide open, basking sharks are like giant mobile sieves filtering out countless tiny creatures on which they feed. This shark is the second largest fish in the world, after the whale shark (pp. 32–33), growing to about 33 ft (10 m) long and weighing over 4.5 tons. Basking sharks often swim at the surface on sunny days with their dorsal fins, and perhaps their snouts or tails out of the water. They are probably more attracted by a concentration of food at the surface than the delights of basking in the sunshine. Unfortunately, here they make easy targets for fishermen who catch them with harpoons or nets. They are caught for their large fins, meat, and the oil in their livers—which may be a quarter of the shark's body weight. Basking sharks also get entangled in nets and ropes, and may be run down by speed boats and jet-skis. To conserve these slow-breeding sharks, they are protected in some areas.

SHARK FISHING
At Achill Island off Irelands's northwest coast, basking sharks were once netted in a bay, then speared with a lance, and dragged ashore. Fishing stopped when the numbers of sharks coming into the bay declined.

Eye

Nostril

Gill arch—water passes through arch and then through a sieve of gill rakers before flowing over the gills and out through the gill slits

OILY MOUTHS
Oil from sharks' livers has been used in cosmetics like lipsticks.

Nostril

Eye

Gill rakers

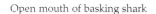
Open mouth of basking shark

0   1,200   2,400   3,600
miles

Distribution of
basking sharks

OPEN MOUTHED
As the basking shark swims along, 400,000
gallons (1.5 million liters) of water flow
through its huge mouth each hour. Drifting
in the water are tiny creatures like baby crabs,
fish eggs, copepods, and arrow worms—all
known as plankton (left)—which are strained
out of the water by hundreds of long bristles,
or gill rakers (pp. 24–25), and trapped in a
layer of slime. After a minute the basking
shark closes its mouth, emptying the water
out through its gill slits before swallowing
its food. Basking sharks may migrate
several thousand miles in search of good
supplies of plankton. In winter, when
plankton becomes scarce in surface waters,
basking sharks may dive as deep as 3,000 ft
(850 m) in search of patches of plankton
that are found there.

SHARK ART ATTACK
This biplane has eye-catching shark
teeth art on its nose and tire covers to
attract attention. Shark faces have also
been used on fighter planes to instill
fear in the enemy—the US Air
Force had them on their Curtiss P-40
Warhawks in the Far East in World
War II, for example.

Angel sharks

IMAGINE RUNNING A STEAMROLLER over a normal-shaped shark—the result would look something like an angel shark. These strange, flattened sharks have extra-large pectoral fins resembling angels' wings. Angel sharks spend much of their lives resting on the seabed or lying in wait for fish or shellfish to move within reach of their snapping, sharp-toothed jaws. They can also swim, using their tails to propel themselves along, just like other sharks. Angel sharks are most active between dusk and dawn, traveling as far as 6 miles (10 km) during the night. There are about 20 species of angel shark that live in shallow coastal waters around the world to depths of over 3,000 ft (1,000 m).

MONK FISH
Ever since the 16th century, angel sharks have also been called "monk fish," because the shape of their heads looks like the hood on a monk's cloak.

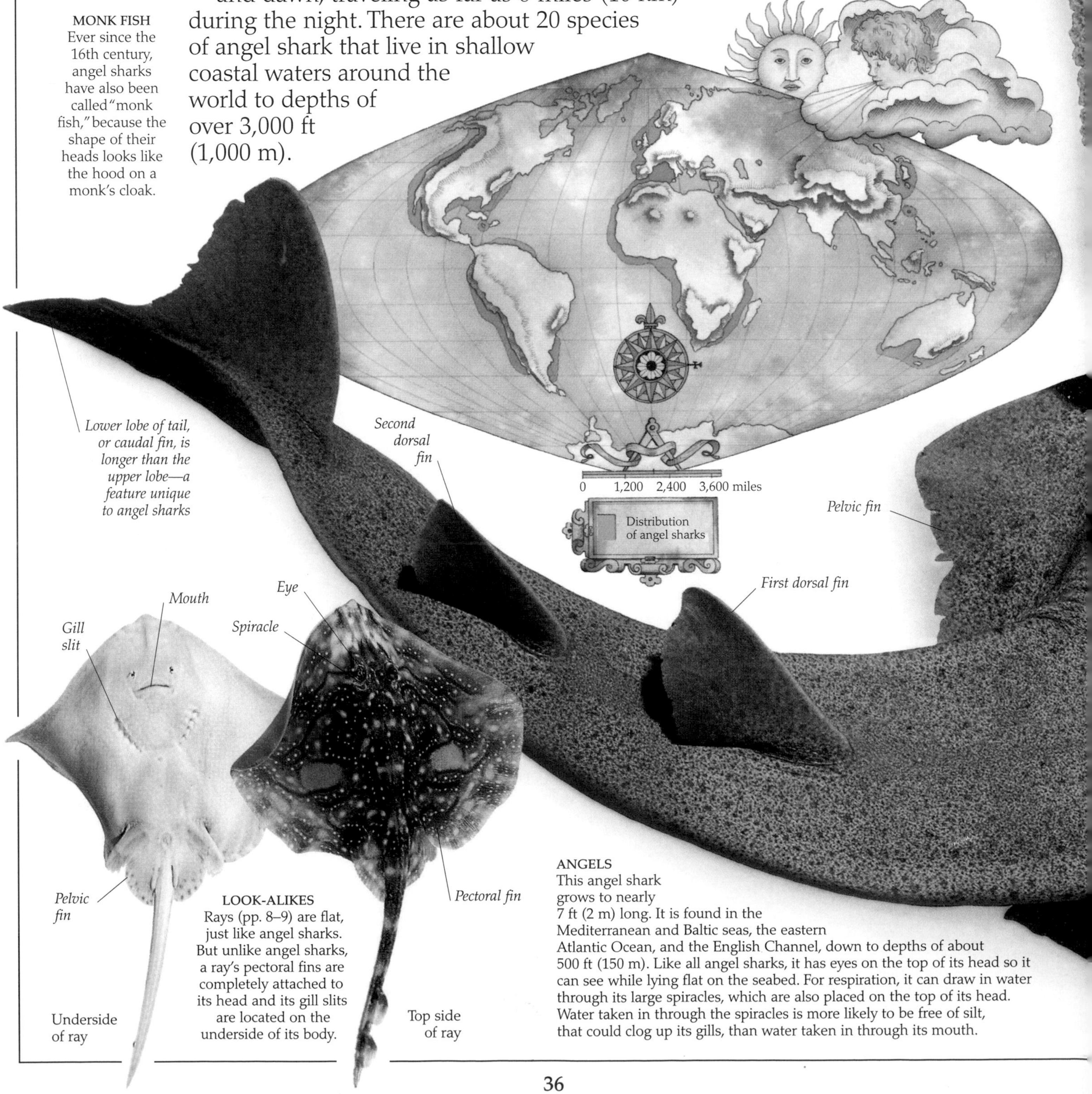

0   1,200   2,400   3,600 miles

Distribution of angel sharks

Lower lobe of tail, or caudal fin, is longer than the upper lobe—a feature unique to angel sharks

Second dorsal fin

Pelvic fin

First dorsal fin

Gill slit

Mouth

Eye

Spiracle

Pelvic fin

LOOK-ALIKES
Rays (pp. 8–9) are flat, just like angel sharks. But unlike angel sharks, a ray's pectoral fins are completely attached to its head and its gill slits are located on the underside of its body.

Underside of ray

Pectoral fin

Top side of ray

ANGELS
This angel shark grows to nearly 7 ft (2 m) long. It is found in the Mediterranean and Baltic seas, the eastern Atlantic Ocean, and the English Channel, down to depths of about 500 ft (150 m). Like all angel sharks, it has eyes on the top of its head so it can see while lying flat on the seabed. For respiration, it can draw in water through its large spiracles, which are also placed on the top of its head. Water taken in through the spiracles is more likely to be free of silt, that could clog up its gills, than water taken in through its mouth.

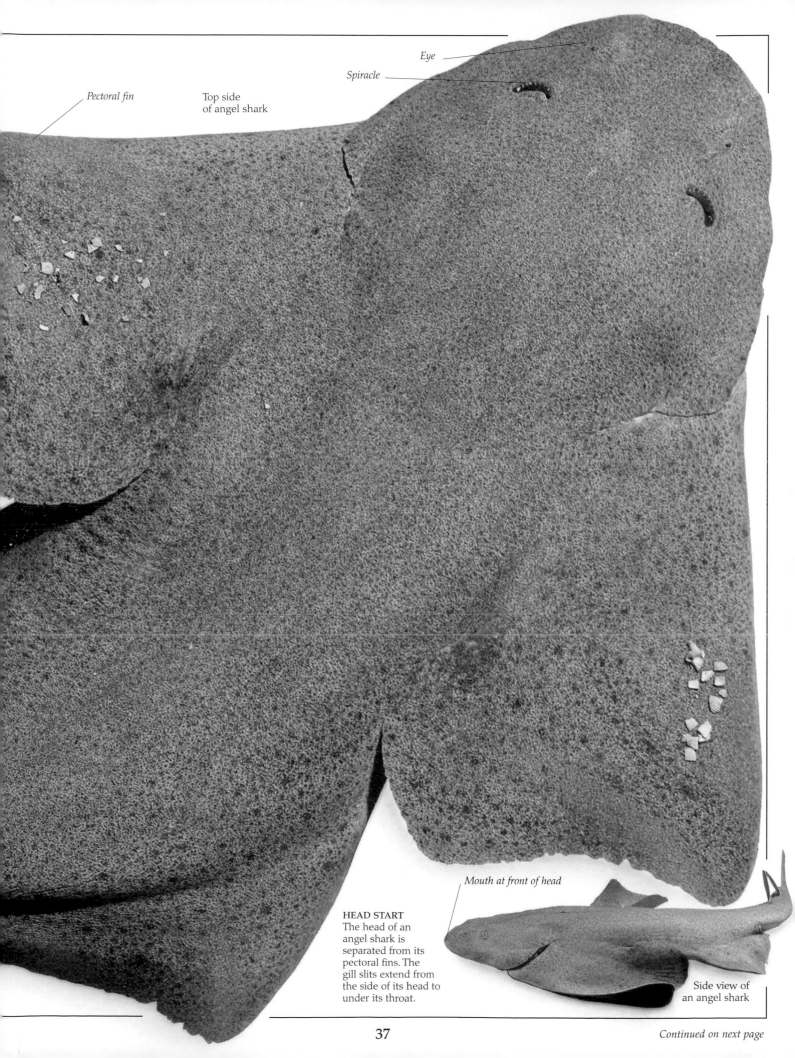

Pectoral fin

Top side
of angel shark

Spiracle

Eye

HEAD START
The head of an
angel shark is
separated from its
pectoral fins. The
gill slits extend from
the side of its head to
under its throat.

Mouth at front of head

Side view of
an angel shark

37

Continued on next page

Japanese wobbegong

Lobe

Barbel

SECRET AGENT
Spies work undercover on secret missions. Some kinds of shark are secretive too, and hide from predators by using camouflage.

ORIENTAL WOBBEGONG
This shark lives along the coasts of Japan, China, Vietnam, the Philippines, and Korea in the western Pacific. It grows to just over 3 ft (1m) in length. Wobbegongs are not normally aggressive, but people have been bitten when they have stepped on a wobbegong by mistake, because they are difficult to see. Fishermen have also been bitten by wobbegongs caught in their nets.

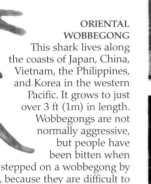

Undercover sharks

Sharks living on the seabed like to hide. The colors and patterns on their skins help these sharks, such as wobbegong, swell, and angel sharks, to be camouflaged, or to blend in with their surroundings. They have blotches, spots, or stripes that make them difficult to see on sand, among rocks, seaweeds, or corals on the seabed. Wobbegongs have elaborate disguises with blotchy skins and lobes on their heads that look like bits of seaweed. Other sharks, like swell sharks, hide in crevices, while angel sharks cover themselves with sand. Why hide if you are a shark with sharp teeth? These undercover sharks often lie in wait for prey, like fish and crabs, to move near, then snap them up. Also, hiding helps small sharks avoid being eaten by larger predators.

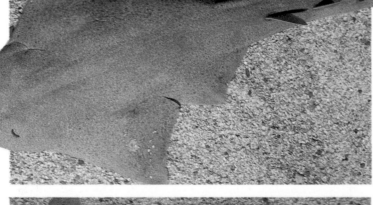

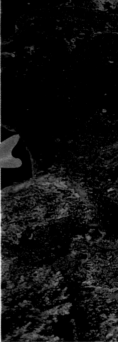

NOW YOU SEE ME, NOW YOU DON'T
It is difficult to see angel sharks (pp. 36–37) lying on the seabed, because they are flattened and their mottled skin looks like sand (top left). To complete their superb disguise, angel sharks shuffle their pectoral fins to bury themselves in the sand (center left). When hiding under a layer of sand, their eyes poke above the surface (bottom left) keeping watch for their prey like fish to swim by. When a fish comes near, the angel shark lunges forward, snapping its jaws shut around it. If divers approach, they may leave their hiding place and swim off. Fishermen catch angel sharks in nets towed across the seabed.

AUSTRALIAN SHARK WITH A BEARD
The tasseled wobbegong's beard has many branched lobes around its mouth, which its prey, such as fish and shrimp, may mistake for seaweed and end up being eaten.

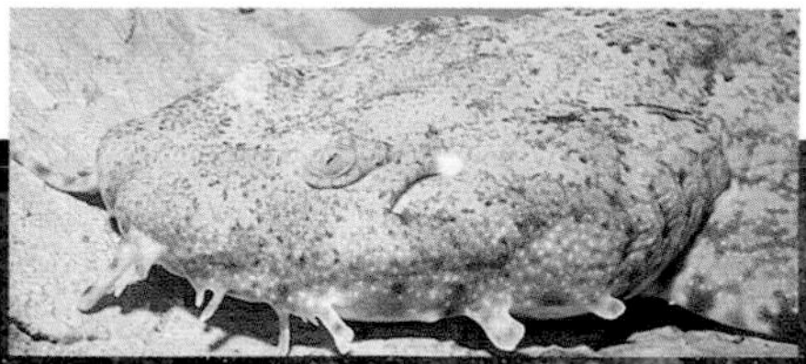

MUG SHOTS
Like a prisoner in mug shots, this ornate wobbegong looks different from different angles—from above (top left) and from the side (bottom left). The wobbegong's disguise works just as well from any direction. Aboriginals of Australia gave wobbegongs their wonderful name.

Predators may not see a swell shark because it is well camouflaged. But if attacked, it gulps down water, swelling up to jam itself into a crevice.

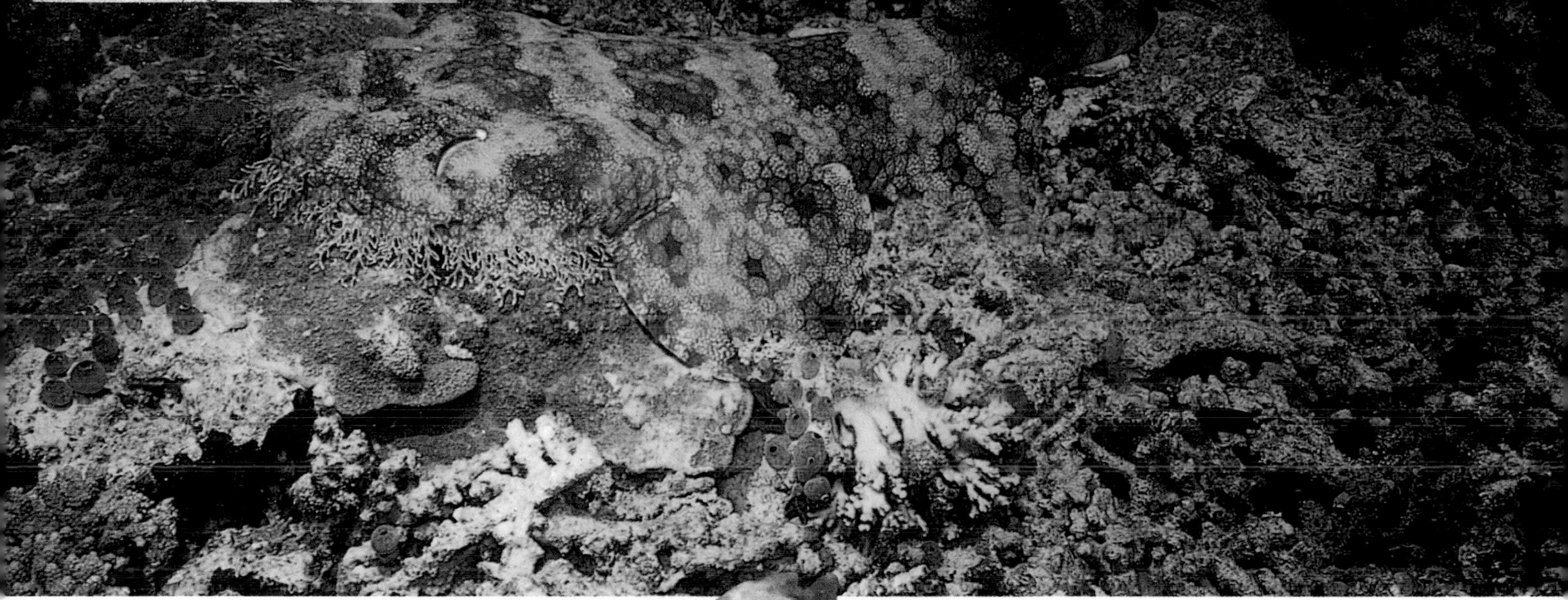

WHERE'S THE TASSELED WOBBEGONG?
Of the seven or so wobbegong species, this one has the most branched lobes, or tassels, on its head. Its beard extends around the mouth and down its chin.

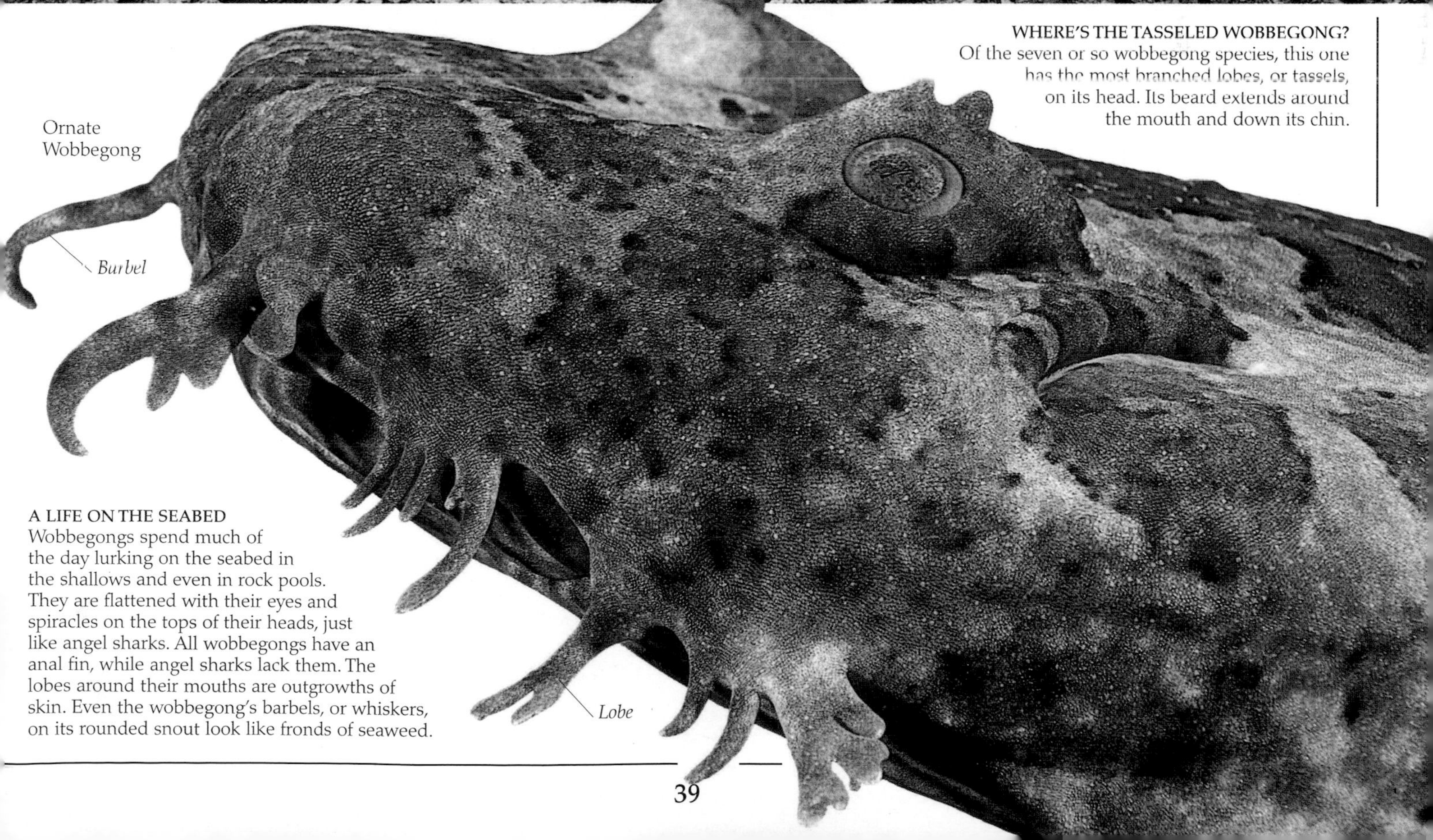

Ornate Wobbegong

Burbel

A LIFE ON THE SEABED
Wobbegongs spend much of the day lurking on the seabed in the shallows and even in rock pools. They are flattened with their eyes and spiracles on the tops of their heads, just like angel sharks. All wobbegongs have an anal fin, while angel sharks lack them. The lobes around their mouths are outgrowths of skin. Even the wobbegong's barbels, or whiskers, on its rounded snout look like fronds of seaweed.

Lobe

Horn sharks

Practising the horn
makes perfect

HORN SHARKS GET THEIR NAME from the two spines on their backs next to each dorsal fin, which look like small horns. The sharks in this group are also called bullheads because they have broad heads with ridges above their eyes. The shape of the head and the presence of an anal fin distinguish horn sharks from spiny dogfish, which also have dorsal spines. There are nine species of horn shark. All are mostly less than 5 ft (1.5 m) long and are found in the Pacific and Indian Oceans, where they live on the seabed in shallow water. Horn sharks swim with slow beats of their tails and push themselves along the bottom with their pectoral fins. Port Jackson sharks can travel long distances, covering 500 miles (850 km) to visit their breeding sites. Because horn sharks are slow, scuba divers sometimes tease them by pulling their tails—they have been known to bite back. Sadly, horn sharks are killed for their spines, used to make jewelry (pp. 60–61).

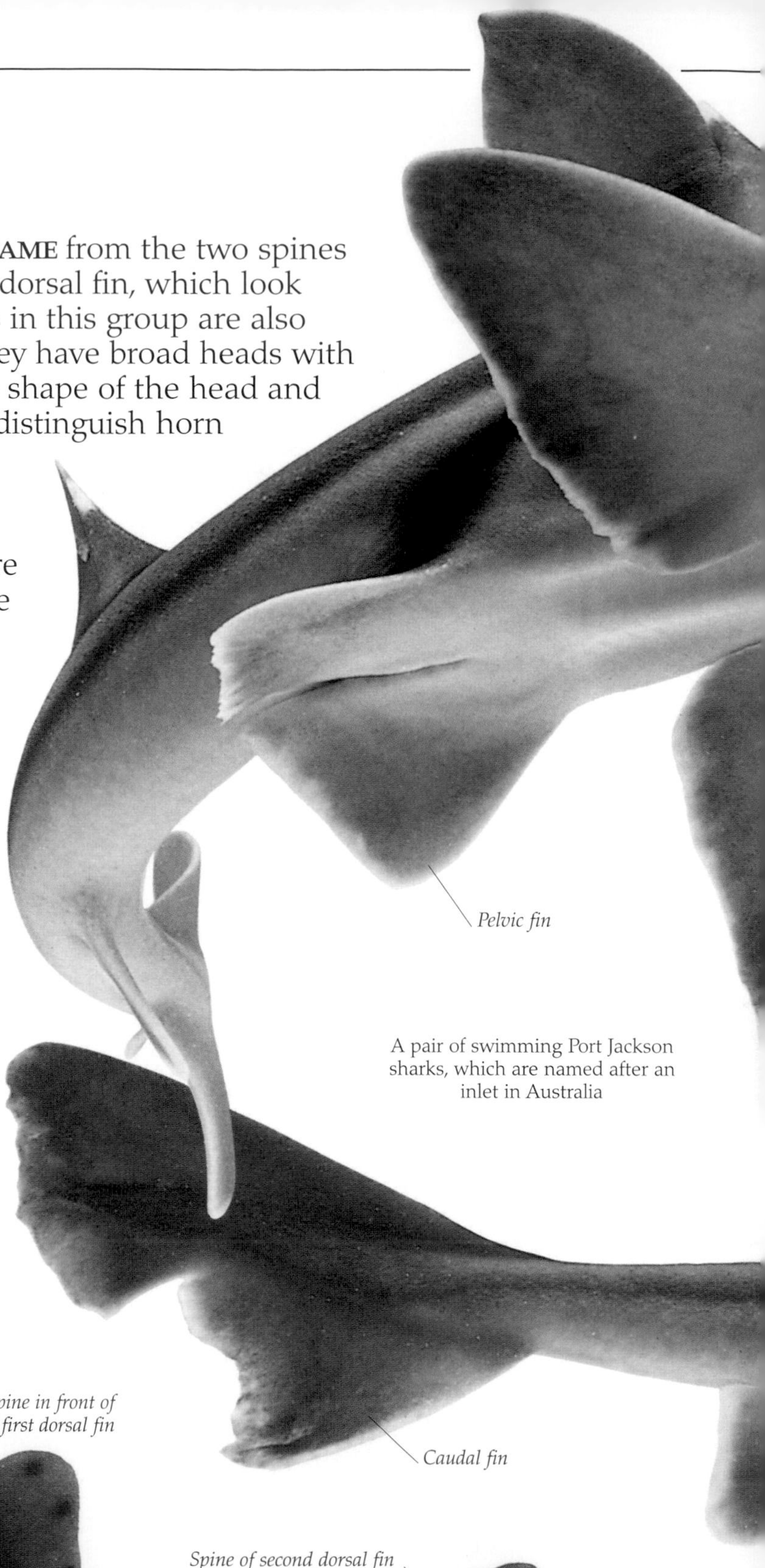

Pelvic fin

A pair of swimming Port Jackson sharks, which are named after an inlet in Australia

HEAP OF HORNS
Port Jackson sharks often share the same spot on the seabed, where they rest in groups during the day. Favorite rest sites are the sandy floors of caves or channels between rocks, which may offer some protection against currents. As many as 16 sharks may share the same resting place. At night they become active searching for food such as sea urchins and starfish.

Spine in front of first dorsal fin

Caudal fin

Spine of second dorsal fin

Typical spotted pattern on skin

Eye

Side view of horn shark

Pelvic fin

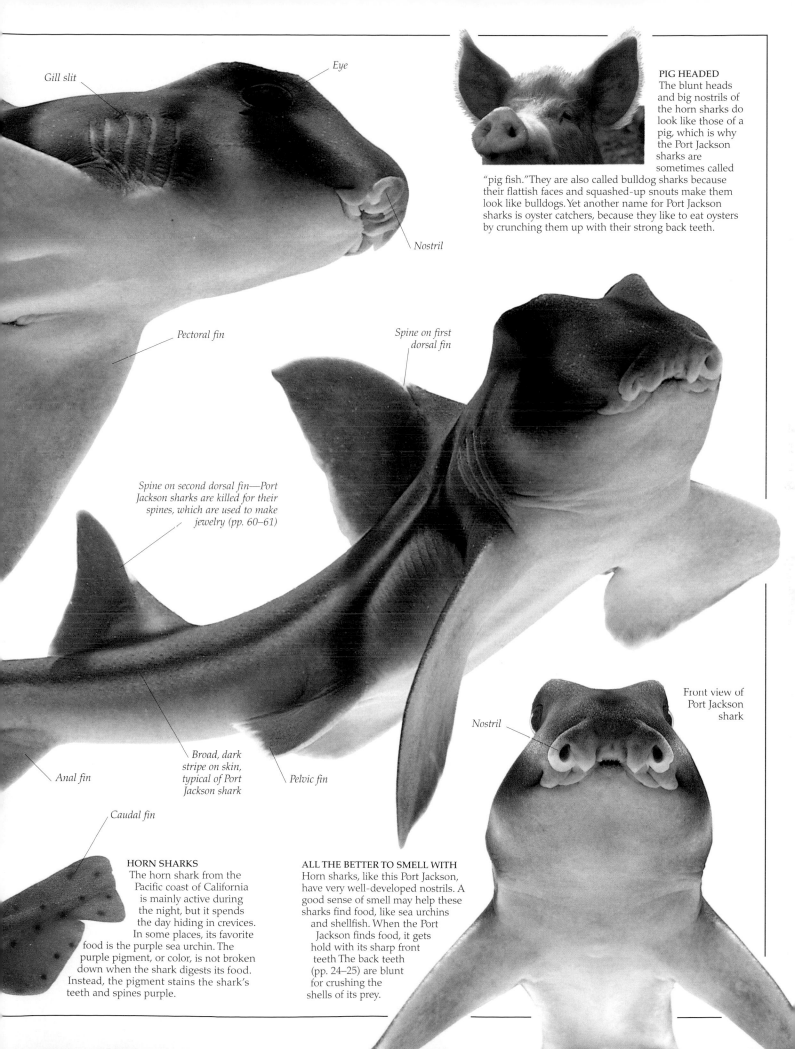

Gill slit

Eye

Nostril

Pectoral fin

Spine on first dorsal fin

Spine on second dorsal fin—Port Jackson sharks are killed for their spines, which are used to make jewelry (pp. 60–61)

Anal fin

Broad, dark stripe on skin, typical of Port Jackson shark

Pelvic fin

Caudal fin

Nostril

Front view of Port Jackson shark

PIG HEADED
The blunt heads and big nostrils of the horn sharks do look like those of a pig, which is why the Port Jackson sharks are sometimes called "pig fish." They are also called bulldog sharks because their flattish faces and squashed-up snouts make them look like bulldogs. Yet another name for Port Jackson sharks is oyster catchers, because they like to eat oysters by crunching them up with their strong back teeth.

HORN SHARKS
The horn shark from the Pacific coast of California is mainly active during the night, but it spends the day hiding in crevices. In some places, its favorite food is the purple sea urchin. The purple pigment, or color, is not broken down when the shark digests its food. Instead, the pigment stains the shark's teeth and spines purple.

ALL THE BETTER TO SMELL WITH
Horn sharks, like this Port Jackson, have very well-developed nostrils. A good sense of smell may help these sharks find food, like sea urchins and shellfish. When the Port Jackson finds food, it gets hold with its sharp front teeth The back teeth (pp. 24–25) are blunt for crushing the shells of its prey.

Head like a hammer

OF ALL THE SHARKS, hammerheads have the strangest shaped heads. Included in the nine species of hammerhead are the bonnetheads, which have small head projections. The winged hammerhead has by far the widest head, which can be half as long as its body. Most hammerhead species live in warm temperate and tropical coastal waters. The scalloped hammerhead is one of the most common species and occurs in warm waters throughout the world. Large schools of scalloped hammerheads congregate in some areas where there are features on the seafloor like undersea peaks, or sea mounts. A hundred of these sharks may form a school with them all swimming in unison. At dusk they swim off on their own to feed (pp. 18–19) and then at dawn they regroup in the same place.

Distribution of hammerheads

Bonnetheads
Winged hammerheads

0   1,200   2,400   3,600   miles

HAMMERHEAD SCHOOLS
There are more females in schools than males, but the reason why they group together is unclear. These large predators have few enemies, so it is unlikely they school for protection. The females compete with each other (often butting one another) to stay in the center of the schools. This may give them a better chance to be courted by the males.

DIFFICULT DIET
Stingrays are the favorite food of the great hammerhead even though their tails are armed with venomous spines, or "stings,". Hammerheads do not seem to mind being stung—one individual had nearly a hundred spines sticking into its mouth and gullet.

Blue spotted stingray

TWO DIFFERENT SHARKS
The shape of the hammerhead's head (top) compared to that of other sharks—like the tope (bottom)—fascinated early naturalists.

A FINE BONNET
Bonnetheads are the smallest of the hammerheads, reaching only 5 ft (1.5 m) long compared to the great hammerhead, which can grow as much as 20 ft (6 m) long. They usually swim together in small groups, but sometimes huge schools of hundreds of sharks congregate near the surface.

Mouth

Gill slit

First dorsal fin

Pectoral fin

WHY A HAMMER?
No one knows why a hammerhead has a hammer-shaped head, but the broad, flattened head may give extra lift to the front of the shark's body as it swims. The two hammerheads (right) differ slightly in that the scalloped one (left) has an indentation in the middle of its head, while the smooth one does not.

Anal fin   Pelvic fin

HEAD ON
As hammerheads swim along, swinging their heads from side to side, they have an excellent all-around view since their eyes are at the tips of their hammers. Their broad heads bear many ampullae of Lorenzini, which sense tiny electric currents generated by their prey (pp.18–19).

Scalloped hammerhead

Weird and wonderful

ONE OF THE WORLD'S most extraordinary sharks, the megamouth was only discovered in 1976. No one had come across this large shark before, although it is over 16 ft (5 m) long and weighs 1,500 lb (680 kg). Since 1976, more than 35 megamouths have been found, including one that was captured alive off the coast of California in 1990. Scientists attached radio tags to this living megamouth so they could follow it (pp. 54–55). The shark spent the day at 450–500 ft (135–150 m) down, feeding on "krill" (shrimplike creatures). After sunset it rose up to within 40 ft (12 m) of the surface following its food source before its descent into the depths at dawn. Another strange shark, the goblin shark, lives in deep water and is rarely seen alive. Other mysteries have been solved. No one knew what caused disk-shaped bites on whales, dolphins, and seals, but the culprits were found to be cookiecutter sharks. Who knows what other weird and wonderful sharks are still to be found deep in the ocean?

Places where the first megamouths were found

BIG MOUTH
Megamouth means "big mouth," a good name for a shark with a 3-ft (1-m) grin. This shark may lure krill into its huge mouth with luminous organs around its lips. The first megamouth was brought up dead from 660 ft (200 m), entangled in the sea anchor of an American naval boat off Hawaii. The second was caught in gill nets (long nets in which fish are trapped) off California; the third was washed up and died on a beach near Perth, Australia; while a fourth was found dead and a fifth alive off the coast of Japan. The sixth was caught and released off the California coast.

Goblin shark

Long snout with sensory pores for detecting prey

Top side of goblin shark's head

Underside of goblin shark's head

REALLY WEIRD
These ugly sharks (above) were first discovered by scientists off the coast of Japan in 1898. They have flabby bodies and are over 10 ft (3 m) long. Not much is known about these rare sharks, that live in deep water down to at least 4,260 ft (1,300 m). The drawing above shows the jaws protruded.

GLOWS IN THE DARK
This is one of the lantern sharks, which live in the oceans' dark depths. They are called lantern sharks because they are luminous, or glow in the dark. Among the world's smallest sharks, they grow to only 8 in (20 cm) long.

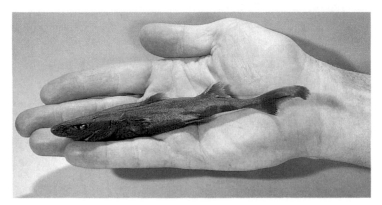

Distribution of cookiecutters

1,200   2,400   3,600 miles

BITE SIZED

Cookiecutters have large teeth for sharks only 20 in (0.5 m) long. The common cookiecutter (one of two species) uses its teeth to cut out chunks of flesh from large fish as well as whales, seals, and dolphins. It may wait for such large animals to come close rather than chasing after them. The cookiecutter forms a suction cup with its lips, then bites and swivels around to take an oval-shaped plug of of flesh. Cookiecutters have also taken bites out of the rubber components of of submarines and undersea cables.

GODDESS OF LIGHT

The cookiecutters' scientific name is *Isistius brasiliensis* after Isis, the Egyptian goddess of light. These sharks have many light organs on their bellies and glow in the dark. This may attract prey like whales to come close enough to be bitten.

BORING BITES
The wounds on this seal were made by a cookiecutter shark biting into its flesh.

Shark artifacts

FOR CENTURIES, people around the world have caught sharks and taken their teeth and skin to make a wide variety of objects, or artifacts. Shark teeth are so sharp that early people were able to make tools and weapons from them. Shark skin is so hard-wearing that it could be used to make shoes, as well as grips or sheaths for swords and daggers (pp. 60–61). Early people who caught sharks had great respect for these magnificent predators. Fishing for sharks with primitive tools was difficult and dangerous, and stories and legends about sharks were common among seafaring and island people. Sharks were even regarded as gods and worshipped on some islands in the Pacific. In comparison, Europeans have few myths about sharks, but they did appear in natural history books (pp. 28–29).

MONKEY BUSINESS
This monkey-head was made by the Aztecs in Mexico. Made of precious stones, its teeth are those of a shark.

Large, serrated tooth, probably from a great white shark (pp. 28–31)

CROWN JEWEL
The 10 shark teeth that went into making this decorative necklace probably came from great white sharks caught by Maoris off the coast of New Zealand. Today's shark-tooth jewelry, made specially for tourists, has contributed to some shark species becoming endangered (pp. 60–61).

Shark skin

Pair of fisherman's shoes, made of shark skin, from India

Shark tooth

Shark-shaped gold weight from Ghana in West Africa

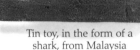

Tin toy, in the form of a shark, from Malaysia

Shark tooth

Tool, tipped with a shark's tooth, for tattooing people's skin, from Kiribati (the Gilbert Islands) in the western Pacific Ocean

18th-century carved wooden drum, with shark-skin-covered top; from the Hawaiian Islands in the Pacific

Wooden rasp, covered in shark skin, from the island of Santa Cruz in the southwest Pacific

Shark skin

Shark-skin-covered grater (below) from the Wallis Islands in the Pacific

Wooden knife (right), with cutting edge made of sharks' teeth, from Greenland

Shark skin

SHARKS IN THE HOME
From ancient times, the skins and teeth of sharks have been used to make a variety of household items. Some shark skins are so rough that they have been used for grating food (left), but if the denticles are removed the soft skin is used like leather for making shoes and belts, or even drums (above). Shark teeth have been used for knives, jewelry, and tools. Other items were made in the shape of a shark because people admired sharks, but, like today, toy sharks were made just for fun.

FISHING AND WORSHIP

Early people often risked their lives trying to catch sharks with primitive harpoons from small boats. Such heroic deeds often became a test of manhood. In some South Pacific islands, boys would go out in canoes to catch sharks for the island kings. They used rattles (right) to make noises in the water to attract sharks to their canoes. Then the sharks would be lured into a noose and killed with a club. The Hawaiian islanders fished for sharks and used both nooses and lines with hooks (below). They also believed that their dead relatives came back to life in the form of animals, such as sharks. These shark spirits would protect them while fishing. On other Pacific islands, sharks were thought of as gods and were never eaten.

Long spear for catching sharks, from the Nicobar Islands, India

Rattle made of coconut shells, for attracting sharks, near Samoa in the South Pacific

Small harpoon for catching sharks, Gambia, West Africa

Shark-tooth necklace from New Zealand

Two hooks for catching sharks—one from Hawaii (right) is made of ivory, while the other (left) is carved in wood, from the Cook Islands in the southwest Pacific

Sea spirit, with a sharklike head, from the Solomon Islands in the southwest Pacific

Solomon Islanders believed a shark-shaped charm would keep large sharks out of their fishing nets (below)

Early 20th-century rattle, for attracting sharks, from Papua New Guinea, an island to the north of Australia

Turn upside down to find a dolphin

BARK PAINTING

Australian Aboriginals painted designs on pieces of bark cut from trees. In their paintings, they often reveal what is inside an animal. In this 20th-century bark painting (left), the painter shows the shark's liver, which has two large lobes.

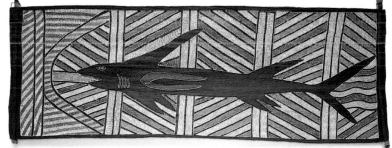

SHARK WEAPONS

Sharp shark teeth were used by people from the Pacific islands as weapons for cutting and slashing their opponents. They made knuckle dusters and gloves (right) as well as swords, using rows of shark teeth as a cutting edge, instead of metal. Shark skin was used in other parts of the world, such as Africa and the Middle East, to make scabbards for protecting metal swords (below).

Shark tooth

Shark tooth

Early Hawaiians packed a punch with this shark-tooth knuckle duster

A warrior from Kiribati would put his fingers into the loops of this glove, to cover his forearm with rows of teeth

Sword used by the Ashanti tribe from Ghana in West Africa

Shark-skin-covered sheath, or scabbard

Gold-plated handle

Shark attack

ATTACK AT SEA
Prisoners, escaping from Devil's Island off Guyana, are attacked by sharks.

MOST SHARKS are not dangerous and leave people alone. There are about 50 to 79 recorded shark attacks on people each year in the world, with up to 10 of these being fatal. People are more likely to die in car accidents or drown in the sea than be killed by a shark. It is dangerous to be in water where there may be sharks: if the water is murky, if you have cut yourself, or if bait has been put out for fish. Pay heed to local shark warning signs and try to swim in areas designated with shark nets.

WOUNDED SEAL
Elephant seals are what many great whites on the California coast like to sink their teeth into. Unlike people, these seals have plenty of energy-rich blubber. The sharks usually grab their prey from behind. Sometimes the seal escapes and manages to reach the beach before the shark attacks again.

FATAL SHARK ATTACK
Most fatal shark attacks occur where people surf, swim, or scuba dive, and where there are large sharks, like the great white, swimming close to shore. Attacks can also occur on people escaping from sinking ships or plane crashes far out to sea. Each year the International Shark Attack File records the numbers of attacks reported.

Each year on average 92 people die by drowning in the sea off Australia's coast …

… while around eight people die from scuba diving accidents …

… and fewer than one person dies from a shark attack.

GREAT WHITE SHARK
Ever since the *Jaws* movies, the great white has had a reputation as a blood-thirsty killer. They do attack and kill people, but this may be because they mistake them for their natural prey. Surfers are at risk near breeding grounds of elephant seals and sea lions, where great whites like to hunt.

WARNING SIGN
To avoid being attacked by sharks, take note of signs like this Australian one. Sharks attack people wading in shallow water.

BULL SHARK
Bull sharks are one of the most dangerous sharks in the world, along with the great white and tiger sharks. The bull shark lives in the warm waters of the world's oceans. It is one of the few sharks that spends time in freshwater, swimming far up rivers such as South America's Amazon and Africa's Zambezi. They can also enter lakes. At 10 ft (3 m) long, they are large enough to tackle a person and are not fussy about what they eat.

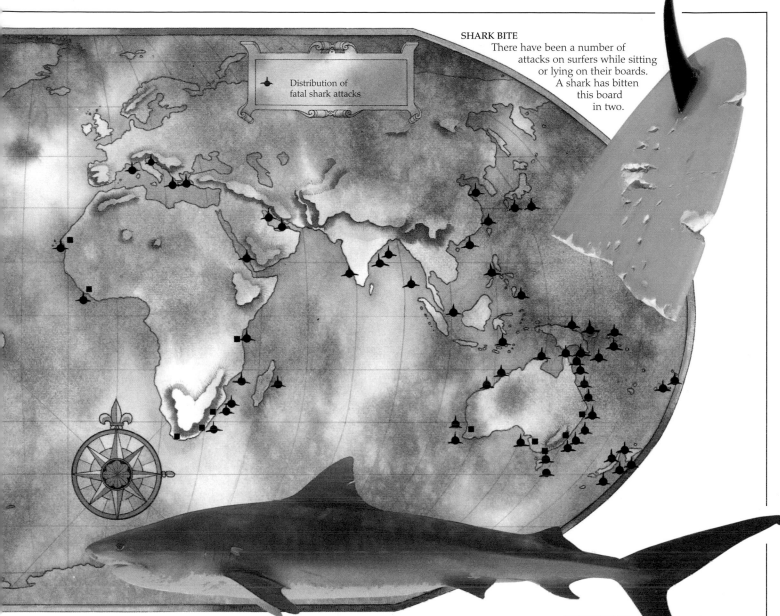

SHARK BITE
There have been a number of attacks on surfers while sitting or lying on their boards. A shark has bitten this board in two.

Distribution of fatal shark attacks

TIGER SHARK
Tiger sharks eat almost anything, from turtles, seals, jellyfish, dolphins, sea birds, sea snakes, and junk like tin cans. They may be tempted to eat any animal, including people, that might make another meal.

DUMMY ATTACK
Wet suits do not protect against shark attacks, as this experiment with dummy shows, nor do colored or patterned wet suits repel sharks.

SHARK'S EYE VIEW
Attacks on surfers occur near seal or sea lion breeding colonies, when surfers have dangled their arms or legs over the edge of their surf boards. Sharks can mistake surfers for seals because they have similar shapes when seen from below.

NORMAL SWIMMING
Gray reef sharks live near coral reefs in the Indian and Pacific oceans and grow to about 8 ft (2.5 m) long. When swimming normally, the back is gently curved and the pectoral fins held straight out from the body.

THREAT POSTURE
If a diver approaches too close or surprises a gray reef shark, it may adopt this threat posture. The shark arches its back and holds its pectoral fins downward. It may also swim around in a figure of eight. If the diver does not swim slowly away, the shark may attack.

Sharks at bay

PEOPLE WHO GO into the water where there may be dangerous sharks run a small risk of being attacked. There is no simple way to keep sharks away from all the places where people paddle, swim, surf, or scuba dive. Shark-proof enclosures have been built but these can only protect small areas because of the large cost. In South Africa and Australia, nets are used along the most popular beaches to trap sharks, but they also trap and kill many harmless sharks, dolphins, rays, and turtles. Drumlines (baited lines with hooks) are also used to capture sharks—and trap fewer harmless animals than nets. Electrical, magnetic, and chemical repellents are all being tested to keep sharks away. A shark that gets aggressive can sometimes be pushed away with a heavy underwater camera. If all else fails, kicking or punching a shark's snout may put it off an attack.

JONAH AND THE?
In the bible story, Jonah was swallowed by a large sea creature, which could have been a shark, rather than a whale.

LIFEGUARDS
Australian lifeguards look out for sharks. If sharks are spotted near a beach, the shark alarm is sounded and swimmers leave the water. The beach may be closed for the rest of the day, if sharks stay in the area. Always follow a lifeguard's advice on safe swimming.

SHARK SHIELD
The Shark Shield is designed to repel sharks by generating an electric field. It may throw the shark's snout into spasm.

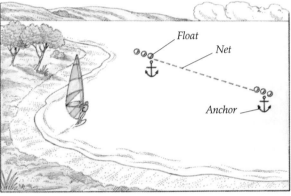
Float — Net — Anchor

IN THE BAG
One way to help people who end up in the sea if a ship sinks or an airplane crashes, is to give them large, inflatable bags. When tested by the US Navy, sharks avoided them, because they could not see any limbs, sense any electric signals, or smell blood or body wastes, which are kept in the bag.

TRAPPED
A shark, trapped in a mesh net off an Australian beach (right), is landed. In the l930s, during a 17-month period, 1,500 sharks were caught by this method. Since then, numbers of sharks have decreased sharply.

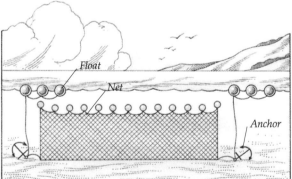
Float — Net — Anchor

NETTING BEACHES
Mesh nets are used to protect the most popular beaches by trapping sharks in the area. The nets do not form a continuous barrier, so sharks may be caught (on both sides of the nets—either swimming toward or away from the beach). Heavy anchors keep the nets on or close to the bottom and floats keep the top of the net suspended in the water. The nets are about 660 ft (200 m) long and 20 ft (6 m) deep. Marker buoys float at the surface so the nets are easily found again. The nets are checked almost every day and dead sea animals removed. After three weeks the nets need to be replaced because they become fouled by seaweed and other marine growth, and so can easily be seen and avoided by sharks. Nets that have become tangled up in storm waves also need to be replaced.

CHAIN WALL
This wall (left) of interlinked chains surrounding an Australian beach prevents any sharks from getting in. Such walls are too costly to protect more than a few miles of beach. Chemical repellants have also been tried but they are not effective, as any substance released around a person in the water disperses too quickly in the waves.

PROTECTED BEACH
Experiments using screens made of bubbles released from air hoses on the seabed have been carried out, but shark nets, as on this Australian beach (above), still seem to offer the best protection.

INVISIBLE BARRIER
Sharks are very sensitive to electric currents and here an invisible electric barrier is being tested. When the current is off (top) the lemon shark swims past, but when the current is switched on (left) the shark turns back to avoid it. Cables and even portable devices that produce electrical pulses to deter sharks have been tested in the sea.

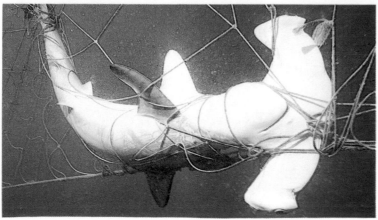

DEATH NETS
Mesh nets, used to protect beaches, kill many sharks each year, like the great white (above) and hammerhead (left). Sharks entangled in nets are not able to swim and suffocate because they cannot keep water flowing over their gills. Up to 1,400 sharks, many of them harmless, as well as dolphins, are caught each year in South African nets.

SHARK REPELLANT
The American scientist Dr. Eugenie Clark discovered that the Moses sole from the Red Sea produces its own shark repellant. When attacked, milky secretions ooze out of pores on its skin, causing the shark to spit it out.

In the cage and out

DIVING SUIT
In the early 19th century, divers wore heavy helmets or hard hats and had air pumped down tubes from the surface. Tall tales were often told about attacks from giant octopuses.

DIVING WITH LARGE predatory sharks can be dangerous, so people who want to get close to sharks, like underwater photographers and film makers, use a strong metal cage to protect themselves. No one sensible would want to be in the water with a great white shark (pp. 28–31), unless protected by a cage. For smaller and less dangerous species, like blue sharks (pp. 56–57), divers sometimes wear chain-mail suits. The chain-mail is sufficiently strong to prevent the shark's teeth from penetrating the skin if it should bite, but bruising can still occur. Divers may also have a cage just to retreat into, should the sharks become aggressive. Because chum (pp. 28–29) and baits are put in the water to attract sharks, they may become excited by the thought of food and snap at the divers. When sharks are being filmed or photographed outside a cage, safety divers should also be present to keep watch for sharks approaching from outside the filmmaker's field of vision.

1 LOWERING THE CAGE INTO WATER
Once the dive boat reaches the right place for great whites, chum is thrown into the water, creating an oily slick, and the metal cage is lowered into the sea.

2 A GREAT WHITE APPROACHES
It may be several days before a great white comes close to the cage, kept on the water's surface by floats. The diver can close the lid of the cage for complete protection, if a shark closes in.

3 A VIEW FROM INSIDE THE CAGE
Baits, like horse meat and tuna, attract the shark near the cage. The bars are close enough together to prevent the great white from biting the photographer, but sharks, attracted by metal, may bite the boat and cage.

IN SHINING ARMOR
Valerie Taylor, one of the early filmmakers, tests the effectiveness of the chain-mail suit. The blue shark (left) is tempted to bite because the sleeve of the suit has been stuffed with pieces of fish. Problems may occur if the shark gets its teeth caught in the chain-mail—in its struggle to get free, it could pull Valerie's glove right off. The suits are also heavy, so swimming is difficult. Chain-mail is still used by people who feed sharks so that divers can photograph and see the sharks more easily. Butchers also use chain-mail gloves (top) to protect their hands from being cut when they slice up meat.

FILMING SHARKS
Australian filmmakers Ron and Valerie Taylor are well known for their work on sharks. Ron Taylor films a white-tipped reef shark taking a bait (right), while a blue shark approaches the camera (below right).

4 GREAT WHITE SWIMS BY
Divers can be shaken off their feet, if these powerful great whites should bump into their cage. Such close-up views of these sharks reveal just how big these awesome creatures really are.

Studying sharks

HMS CHALLENGER
This British research vessel took 19th-century naturalists to the Atlantic, Pacific, and Indian oceans, where all kinds of marine life, including sharks, were collected.

IN THE WILD, it is difficult to study sharks because they constantly move around, swim too fast, and dive too deep for divers to keep up with them. Some sharks, like hammerheads, are even scared away by bubbles produced by scuba divers. To follow sharks, scientists catch them and attach special tags to their fins. When the sharks are released, scientists can keep track of them by picking up signals with a receiver or via a satellite. Great care is taken to keep sharks alive when they are caught for tagging and other studies. Certain types of shark are captured and placed in aquariums for observation (pp. 62–63).

SATELLITE TRANSMITTING DEVICE
By tracking sharks by satellite, scientists have discovered that the great white swims long distances each year, such as across the Indian Ocean.

data store

Seabed retriever logging shark presence

STUDYING LEMONS
Dr. Samuel Gruber has studied lemon sharks in the Bahamas for more than 10 years. They do not mind being handled and do not need to swim to breathe, so they can be kept still while scientists make their observations. In this experiment (right), a substance is being injected into the shark to show how fast it can grow. Young lemons too can have tiny tags inserted in their dorsal fins and are identified later by their own personal code number.

Propeller measuring a shark's swimming speed is attached to fin of a mako shark

GETTING UP A SHARK'S NOSE
American scientist Dr. Samuel Gruber checks the flow of water through this nurse shark's nose. Scientists have to be careful because, although nurse sharks are normally docile, they can give a nasty bite (pp. 18–19).

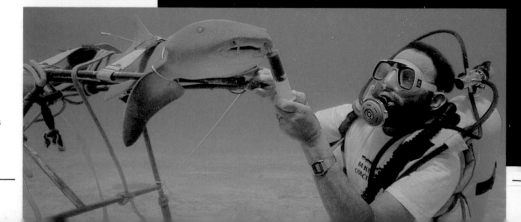

SCIENTISTS' FAVORITE
Lemon sharks are one of the easiest sharks to study, both in aquariums and in the sea. A young lemon shark (left) attacks her food. When she eats, she shakes her head vigorously, creating a large amount of debris in the aquarium's water.

TAGGING TIGERS
Scientists tag a small tiger shark in the Bahamas (top). Sometimes sharks need to be revived after this, so a diver (above) is pushing a large tiger shark along to keep water flowing over its gills.

KEEPING DRY

To go underwater without getting wet, American naturalist Prof. W. Beebe (1877– 1962) used this bathysphere in the 1930s to reach a depth of 3,300 ft (1,000 m). Sharks, as deep as 12,000 ft (3,600 m), are attracted by bait.

THE FRILL OF IT ALL
Three of these strange sharks (below) were caught off Japan in deep water during the 1870s' *Challenger* expedition.

Frilled shark

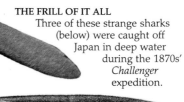

Sixth gill slit—most sharks have only five

Tagging sharks

ANGLERS CAN HELP SCIENTISTS find out where sharks go and how fast they grow by measuring, tagging, and releasing them. Tens of thousands of sharks have been tagged since the 1950s, off the coasts of the US and Australia, as well as the UK and Africa. A few tags are recovered when fishermen catch these sharks again. The record is for a male Australian tope, which was first tagged in 1951 and recaptured in 1986, 130 miles (214 km) from its original release site. Its length had increased by 7 in (17 cm). Blue sharks are among the greatest ocean travelers. One tagged near New York was caught 16 months later off Brazil, 3,600 miles (6,000 km) away, while another tagged off the UK's Devon coast was recaptured off Brazil, 4,200 miles (7,000 km) away.

Australian certificate (top), and card (bottom) for details of captured shark

Two Australian applicators with nylon and plastic tags

Return address

Tag

Metal tip pierces shark's skin

Where blue sharks have been tagged, released, and recaptured

Cornwall, UK

West Africa

Eastern Seaboard, US

0   600   1,200   1,800 MILES

BIRD RINGING
Ringing bands around young birds' legs gives information on migration—just as tags do for sharks—if they are caught again.

Bait

1 TAGGING/RELEASING SHARKS
Like most sharks, blue sharks have an excellent sense of smell and are attracted to boats by dangling a chum bag containing smelly, salted fish over the side. The chum's oil spreads out in a thin film over the water's surface, attracting sharks from a great distance. The shark hooks are baited with freshly caught mackerel and the fishing lines are let out to depths of 40–60 ft (12–18 m).

2 HOOKED
Attracted by the oil and blood, the blue shark has taken the bait.

3 REELING IN
The shark is reeled in near the boat, very carefully, so as not to damage the shark.

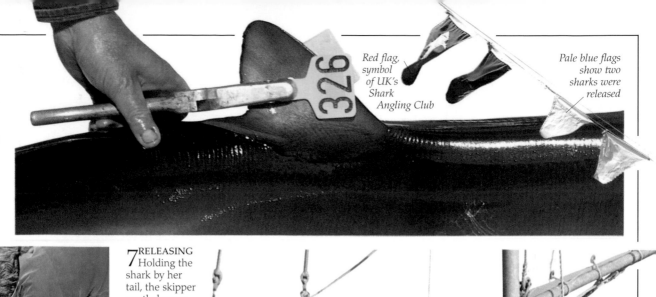

6 TAGGING DORSAL FIN

The tag is made of strong metal that will not corrode in seawater and cause the plastic numbered tag to drop out. On the reverse side of the tag is an address to where the tag can be sent, should another angler or fisherman catch the tagged shark again in another part of the world.

Red flag, symbol of UK's Shark Angling Club

Pale blue flags show two sharks were released

7 RELEASING

Holding the shark by her tail, the skipper gently lowers her back into the sea. Once in the water, the shark swims away as fast as she can.

5 HOLDING THE SHARK DOWN

This female blue shark is 5 ft (1.5 m) long and weighs about 50 1b (22.5 kg). The skipper holds her down and gets ready to insert the tag. The shark can tolerate being out of the water for only a few minutes, so he has to work quickly to put the tag into her dorsal fin. Buckets of saltwater are thrown onto the shark to help keep her alive. In other tagging studies, the shark is brought close to the boat and not landed to keep from damaging it. Then a pole is used to stick the tag into the shark (pp. 28–29).

4 THRESHING SHARK

The skipper begins to haul the threshing shark in, but it fights every bit of the way.

Shark overkill

PEOPLE KILL SHARKS for their meat, fins, skin, and liver oil, as well as for pure sport. Sport fishing can reduce numbers of sharks locally, but the biggest threat to sharks is overfishing worldwide. Sharks, caught on long lines and in fishing nets, are often thrown back into the sea dead, because it is other fish hauled in at the same time that are wanted. Sometimes, just the shark's fins are removed and its body thrown back. Sharks are also killed each year in nets to protect swimmers. Compared to bony fish, sharks have a much slower rate of reproduction and take a long time to mature. If too many are killed, their numbers may never recover. Efforts are now being made to protect sharks by creating reserves, restricting numbers caught, and banning fishing.

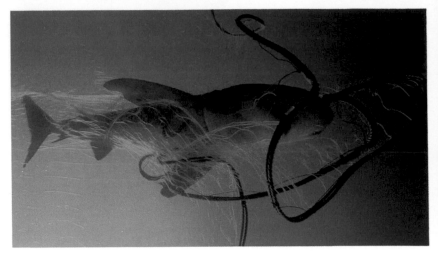

ANGLING
Angling is a popular sport. Fast, strong sharks represent a big challenge. Today, angling clubs are becoming more aware of conservation and some are restricting the size of shark that can be landed. Increasingly, anglers are encouraged to release sharks instead of killing them (pp. 56–57).

WALLS OF DEATH
Drift nets (top), some 50 ft (15 m) deep and many miles long, are used to catch fish. The nets are so fine that fish do not see them and become trapped in the mesh. Sharks, like this oceanic white-tipped shark (above), are easily caught, along with seabirds, turtles, and dolphins.

WHITE DEATH
For many anglers, the great white (above) is the ultimate trophy. People are frightened of great whites and so kill them, but among the sea's predators, these sharks are important in keeping the natural balance in the ocean. Great whites are protected in many countries where hunting these sharks is banned. International trade in shark body parts, such as teeth and jaws, is also controlled.

SPORT OR SLAUGHTER
To show just how many sharks were killed, this hunter's boat (left) showed a collection of the victims' jaws.

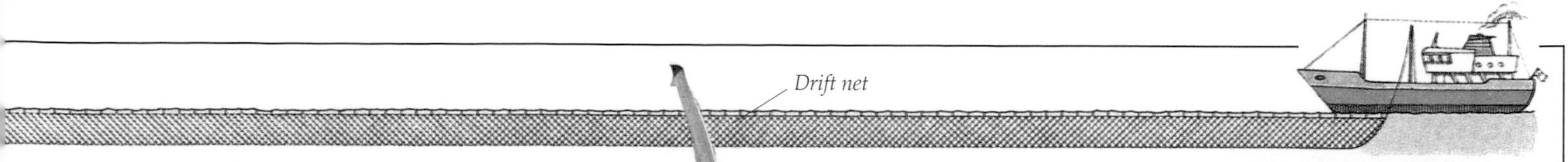

Drift net

THRASHED THRESHER
Thresher sharks (left) are heavily fished in both the Pacific and Indian oceans. They are caught with long lines and gill nets. Landing a thresher can be dangerous, especially if they lash out with their tails. Sometimes their tails get hooked on long lines.

SAD END FOR A TIGER
The tiger shark (right) was killed in an angling competition in Florida. Competitions to catch big sharks were popular in the past, but now conservation-minded anglers tag and release the sharks they catch.

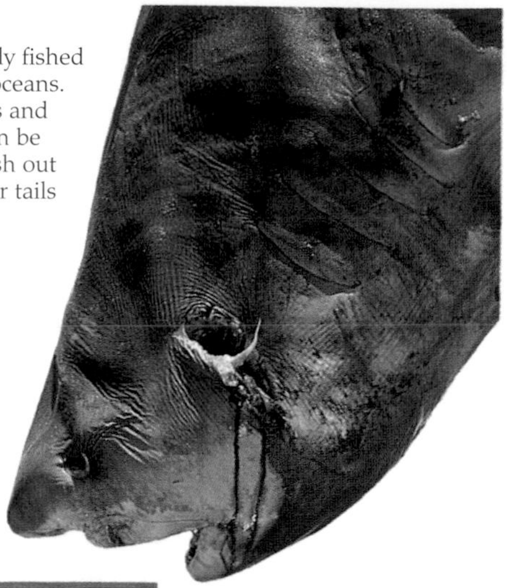

FISHING FOR FOOD
In developing countries, people depend on shark meat for protein. In other countries, shark is a luxury food in restaurants. Whether we choose to eat shark or not, it is important that shark fishing is controlled. If not, these fascinating creatures could disappear from the world's oceans.

Cutting up sharks for meat

DRYING FINS
Shark fins are used in Chinese cooking for delicacies like shark fin soup. Because the fins can be dried, they are much easier to market than shark meat, which has to be sold quickly or processed.

Shark fins drying

FINNING
These Japanese fishermen on a boat in the Pacific Ocean are cutting the fins off sharks caught in drift nets. They throw the rest of the shark back in the sea. Fins of many different kinds of shark are removed, sometimes when the animals are still alive. When thrown back in the sea, they take a long time to die. Without their fins, they are not able to swim properly and may be torn apart by other sharks.

Use and abuse

PEOPLE HAVE FOUND A USE for almost every part of a shark's body. The tough skin can be turned into leather, the teeth into jewelry, the jaws into souvenirs, the carcass into fertilizers, the fins into soup, the flesh eaten, and the oil from the liver used in industry, medicines, and cosmetics. Human exploitation of wild animals like sharks can cause a serious decline in numbers, if more animals are killed than can be replaced by the birth and survival of the young. Sharks are especially at risk because they are slow to reproduce. It is hard to put sensible limits on the numbers of shark that can safely be fished because so little is known about them. Today, sharks are mainly exploited for their meat and fins and demand for shark meat will probably continue as the human population increases. If fewer people were to use products derived from sharks, their future would be more secure. Otherwise, the effect on the natural balance in the oceans could prove to be disastrous.

NAPOLEON AND THE SHARK
Sailors feared and disliked sharks. Here, the French emperor Napoleon (1769–1821) watches a shark being killed, during his journey into exile on the remote Atlantic island of St. Helena.

SHARK TEETH
These pendants are made from the teeth of the great white shark. Misguided people think that wearing shark tooth pendants make them look as fierce as a great white.

GETTING A GRIP
This sword handle, covered with rough shark skin, gives a swordsman a secure grip.

In battle, a bloody handle could still be gripped

The shark skin on the handle of this British Royal Artillery officer's sword has been dyed

Rough ray skin under black cord

SAMURAI SWORD
This 19th-century sword once belonged to a Samurai warrior from Japan. Its handle is covered with unpolished ray skin, while the sheath is made of the polished and lacquered skin of a ray (pp. 8–9).

Lacquered ray-skin-covered sheath

Curved ivory handle

PERSIAN DAGGER
The sheath of this 19th-century Persian dagger is covered in ray skin. A flowery design has been painted onto the lacquered skin.

Outside of each door decorated with double happiness characters

BOX OF HAPPINESS
Fine shark skin, or leather, was used to cover this early 20th-century rectangular box from Korea. The leather is smooth because the denticles, or small teeth, have been highly polished, then lacquered, and dyed dark green. Shagreen—rough, unpolished shark skin—is used as an abrasive, like sandpaper, for polishing wood.

SHARK REMAINS
These two hammerheads (pp. 42–43) were caught off the coast of the Baja Peninsula in western Mexico. In this poor area, their meat was probably used for food and their skin for making into leather goods, such as wallets and belts.

SHARK AND CHIPS

Much of the fish sold in British fish and chip shops is, in fact, spiny dogfish (pp. 22–23), one of the most abundant and heavily fished kinds of shark. Many kinds of shark are given a different name when sold for meat—dogfish is disguised as "rock salmon" in Britain. In the past, people did not like to eat shark because they thought sharks ate the bodies of dead sailors. Sadly, shark steaks are becoming a fashionable delicacy in some restaurants.

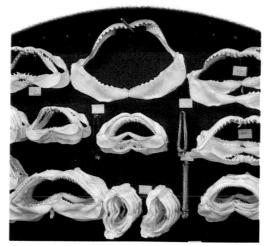

JAWS FOR SALE

Many sharks are killed and their jaws sold to tourists as souvenirs. Jaws of large sharks, like the great white (pp. 28–31), fetch high prices. The sale of great white jaws is now banned in South Africa.

HEADLESS CORPSE

This shark was killed for sport and had its head cut off so its jaws could be removed. Shark jaws are popular trophies in the same way that hunters show off the head and horns of deer they have shot.

Polished, lacquered ray skin

SHARK LIVER OIL PILLS

In some countries people believe that shark oil can cure all kinds of ills. Shark oil is composed of many different substances, including vitamin A, but this vitamin can now be made artificially.

A cluster of shark liver oil pills

Two bowls and a can of an oriental delicacy—shark fin soup

SHARK FIN SOUP

The cartilaginous fibers in shark fins are made into soup, which some people regard as a delicacy. The dried fins are soaked and repeatedly boiled to extract the mass of gelatinous fibers. Many other ingredients are then added to these noodlelike fibers to give the soup some taste.

SKIN CARE

Shark oil is used in costly skin creams that are meant to prevent wrinkles and signs of aging. But other creams based on natural plant oils are just as effective.

Save the shark!

SHARKS HAVE A BAD reputation as blood-thirsty killers. But only a few kinds of shark are dangerous (pp. 48–49) and attacks on people are rare. Other animals like tigers, and even elephants, which also occasionally kill people, are more popular. People need to be concerned about sharks because they are increasingly threatened by overfishing (pp. 58–59). Some sharks, like lemon sharks in Florida, also suffer because of the destruction of mangrove swamps, which are important nurseries for their pups. To begin to like sharks, people need to learn all about them. By visiting an aquarium, everyone can see the grace and beauty of sharks. Good swimmers can learn to snorkel and scuba dive, and may be lucky enough to see sharks in the sea. In some parts of California scuba divers are taken on trips to specific places where they can observe truly wild sharks.

MAD ON SHARKS
This crazy sculpture of a blue shark on the roof of a house near Oxford, England, shows just how much some people like sharks.

Making sketches of various sharks in an aquarium

TANKS FOR THE VIEW
Seeing sharks come within inches of your nose is a great thrill, even if there is a glass wall in between (right). Not all kinds of shark can be kept in aquariums. Smaller sharks, such as smooth-hounds (pp. 14–15) are the easiest. However, as aquariums are getting larger tanks and becoming more skilled at handling sharks, more unusual species are on view. The Okinawa Churaumi Aquarium in Japan keeps whale sharks, and young great white sharks are sometimes keep in the Monterey Bay Aquarium, in California.

Face to face with a shark (right) and feeding time at the aquarium (far right)

RECORDING SKATE AND RAY EGG CASES

Like sharks, certain kinds of ray and skate are also under threat. The UK-based conservation charity, the Shark Trust, has a simple way for people to help monitor ray and skate around the British coast. Recording empty egg cases that wash up on beaches may give clues as to the whereabouts of skate and ray nursery grounds. This may allow these important areas to be protected.

LEARNING ABOUT SHARKS

Join a conservation organization that works to help protect marine life in the oceans and seas. Look out for informative articles in wildlife magazines and for other books about sharks. There are also interesting underwater programs on television which, unlike the scary *Jaws* movies, tell the real story about sharks. Aim to volunteer to help marine biologists in their research programs, like the Earthwatch research in the Bahamas in the Caribbean. There is still so much more to be discovered about sharks.

A sketch of a classic requiem shark, with its streamlined body and highly efficient system of movement that complements its predatory lifestyle

A typical mackerel shark, which is stouter than a requiem shark

Sketching sharks can be fun as well as useful

SHARKS ON FILE

Visiting aquariums, keeping a shark notebook, drawing pictures of sharks, or copying them from photographs, are good ways of seeing how many different kinds of shark there are. Compare the sharks' colors, variety of skin patterns, and the different body shapes. Eventually, a valuable shark information file can be built up. Note down the size, diet, natural habitat, and how the various sharks differ. On sketches, label their external features, like fins, gill slits, eyes, and mouth. With some effort, anyone can become more of an expert on sharks.

Noting down your observations can help build up a valuable shark information file

Pastels

Pencils

Did you know?

FASCINATING FACTS

Natives of some Pacific islands once worshipped sharks as gods, and would therefore never consider eating their meat.

Like many mammals, including humans, sharks have large hearts with four separate chambers.

Sharks often have fantastically powerful jaws; some are capable of exerting 130 lb (60 kg) of pressure per tooth when they bite.

Tiger shark's jaw

A shark's specialized intestine (the spiral valve) provides a relatively large surface area in a limited space. It slows up digestion considerably, though, so a meal can take anything up to four days to digest.

Galapagos shark

The Galapagos shark lives mostly around tropical reefs but may swim long distances between islands.

A shark dart is a crude form of protection against sharks. The dart is fired into a shark and releases carbon dioxide, causing the shark to float to the surface and die.

Great white shark's tooth

Boat builders in some parts of Africa rub the wood of a new craft with hammerhead oil in the belief that it will ensure fair winds and successful voyages.

A shark has an extremely stretchy, U-shaped stomach that can expand to accommodate an enormous meal, which will last the animal several days.

Sharks in captivity can grow faster than they would in the wild because they are fed well and do not need to hunt.

A large part of a shark's brain is linked to its sense of smell; sharks can detect one part of scent in 10 billion parts of water.

The teeth of a tiger shark are strong enough to crunch through a turtle's bones and shell.

About 38 million sharks are caught each year for the fin trade.

Model of *cladoselache*, an ancient shark

Since they first appeared millions of years ago, sharks have probably changed less in evolutionary terms than any other vertebrate.

In 17th-century France, shark brain was eaten to ease the pain of childbirth. It was also combined with white wine and taken for kidney stones.

On average, a shark can survive on 0.5–3 per cent of its body weight per day. Faster, more active sharks need to eat more than slower, sluggish sharks.

Giving his work the title *The Physical Impossibility of Death in the Mind of Someone Living,* English artist Damien Hirst exhibited an Australian tiger shark preserved in green embalming fluid inside a steel and glass tank.

Unidentified bite marks were discovered on the rubber coating of listening devices on submarines belonging to the US Navy. The marks turned out to be made by the cookiecutter sharks.

The meat of sharks is still widely eaten (such as dogfish and even porbeagles) but that of the Greenland shark is inedible until left to rot. It is a delicacy in Iceland despite a strong flavor of ammonia.

More than twice as durable as conventional leather, shark skin has been used in the same way to make shoes, handbags, and belts.

Hawksbill turtle

Upper tail (caudal) lobe

Aside from people, a shark's greatest enemy is another shark; most sharks will happily eat any of their relations, including their own species.

Shark skin has been used to buff marble to a high shine and to give a smooth finish to wood.

Game fishermen often release sharks after they catch them.

In some shark species, the female continues to produce eggs when she's pregnant, and the developing sharks eat them. With the sand tiger (gray nurse shark), the first pup to develop in each uterus consumes its developing siblings.

A shark is able to detect an electrical field of only 100-millionth of a volt.

There are only a few records of sharks getting cancer. This has led to studies in the hope of finding anticancer substances in shark cartilage and other tissues. However, taking ground-up shark cartilage is unlikely to have any benefit.

One of the latest antishark devices is a battery-operated machine designed to fasten onto water craft (including surfboards) and send out electrical impulses. These cause enough distress to approaching sharks to repel them.

Brain-to-weight ratios suggest some kinds of shark are of similar intelligence to birds and mammals. Sharks can be trained in exchange for food rewards; lemon sharks were trained to push a target with their snouts and nurse sharks to bring rings.

Thresher shark

After mating, some female sharks can retain the male sperm in their bodies for use when they are ready to reproduce—even if that doesn't happen until the next season.

Some species of shark can detect light one-tenth as bright as the average person can see. Deep-water sharks have especially large eyes to help them penetrate the gloom.

Reef sharks feeding on surgeon fish

Some kinds of shark are fussy eaters; they sometimes take a sample bite out of their prey—or just sink their teeth in to get a taste—before they begin to feed properly. If they don't like the taste, they will spit out the bite and move on.

When there's a large quantity of food available, sharks will gather around it in an uncontrolled feeding frenzy, during which they will bite anything that comes near, including each other.

The hammerhead's mouth is located under its head.

Hammerhead shark

The hammerhead shark eats stingrays, swallowing them whole in spite of their poisonous spine. If the sting becomes embedded in the shark's jaw, its teeth may grow abnormally.

Sharks prefer to prey on injured or diseased weakened creatures than on strong ones that will fight back. Sharks are also scavengers. The great white sometimes feasts on whale carcasses.

Sharks can easily mistake reflections from metal or sparkly stones for the sheen of fish scales. Don't wear jewelry when you're swimming where sharks have been seen!

Artificial skin from shark cartilage has been used to treat burns.

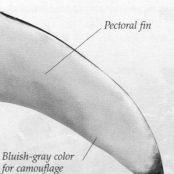

Great white shark

Pectoral fin

Bluish-gray color for camouflage

In order to feed, cookiecutter sharks travel from the bottom of the sea to the surface—a round trip of over 4 miles (7 km).

Shark liver oil contains squalene, which is used in cosmetics and alternative medicine.

QUESTIONS AND ANSWERS

Pack of reef sharks hunting at night

Q How can swimmers lessen their chances of attack?

A Sharks tend to attack people who are swimming on their own, so swimmers should always stay in a group. They should also steer clear of waters where seals, sea lions, or large schools of fish are often seen, since sharks are attracted to these creatures; similarly, it's a good idea to give porpoises a wide berth, since they have a similar diet to sharks and tend to hunt in the same places. People who are bleeding, even from a small cut anywhere on their body, should remain on the beach, since sharks can sense even the tiniest amount of blood in the water. They are also very sensitive to bodily waste, so it's dangerous, as well as unhygienic, to use the sea as a toilet.

Q Do sharks exist together in partnerships or social relationships?

A There is still a great deal scientists haven't discovered about the mating habits and social lives of sharks, but some species, such as the whitetip reef shark, are known to hunt in groups. Great white sharks are sometimes found in pairs and small groups at feeding sites in which there appears to be a pecking order, with the larger sharks dominating the smaller sharks.

Q Are sharks territorial?

A Most sharks do not stay in the same place, but wander freely through the ocean. Some species break the pattern and become attached to a particular area; gray reef sharks, for example, establish a base and patrol it regularly. Similarly, whitetip sharks frequently stay in the same area for extended periods of time, but they are not known to defend their chosen territory.

Q Are sharks ever found in fresh-water?

A Most sharks live in the ocean but the bull shark, otherwise known as the Zambezi River shark, may swim into estuaries and up rivers. It has a sophisticated regulatory system that allows it to adjust to dramatic changes in salt level. Although this shark is found only in warm latitudes, it is capable of swimming far up large rivers and can survive in lakes. As a

result it comes into closer contact with humans than other sharks. The bull shark is a large predator that sometimes attacks humans.

Q In what conditions is a shark attack on a person most likely to occur?

A The majority of shark attacks occur where people like to paddle and swim. This is often during the summer months when the water may be warmer. Attacks are most likely to take place in less than 7 ft (2 m) of calm water, and within a comparatively short distance of the water's edge—about 35 ft (10 m). Particularly hazardous locations are protected inlets, channels where the water suddenly gets deeper, places where garbage is dumped, and the immediate area around docks, quays, and wharfs, especially where people fish.

Seals can attract hungry sharks and so should be avoided by swimmers.

Q Is each different species of shark known by the same name in every part of the world?

A While Latin names are standard everywhere, common names sometimes vary widely. The bull shark (*Carcharhinus leucas*), for example, has an unusually varied collection of common names, perhaps because it is found in a number of different types of habitat. Included in its many names are: Zambezi River shark, Lake Nicaragua shark, Ganges River shark, shovel-nose shark, slipway gray shark, square-nose shark, and Van Rooyen's shark.

Bull shark or Zambezi River shark

RECORD BREAKERS

Whale shark being filmed by a diver

HARD TO FIND
The fact that the megamouth shark was discovered as recently as 1976, and only about 37 sightings have been documented up to 2007, suggests that this is one of the rarest species.

CHAMPION SWIMMER
The fastest-moving sharks are the blue and the mako. The blue shark can reach speeds up to 43 mph (69 km/h), but only in short bursts; their normal speed is about 7 mph (11 km/h).

INTREPID TRAVELER
The most widely traveled species is the blue shark, which commonly migrates up to 2,000 miles (3,000 km). Atlantic blues may do a round trip of up to 10,000 miles (17,000 km). A great white shark called Nicole was tracked using a satellite tag. She swam 6,800 miles (11,000 km) across the Indian Ocean.

LONGEST TAIL
Thresher sharks have tails about as long as their bodies.

MURKY DEPTHS
The deepest level at which sharks have been sighted is around 13,000 ft (4,000 m). Only a few sharks live at such depths because there is so little for them to eat.

Nurse shark

HOMEBODY
The least enthusiastic traveler is the nurse shark, which remains in the same small section of reef for its entire life.

OLD MAN OF THE SEA
Most sharks live for 20 to 30 years, but some reach 80. Experts suspect that the large, slow whale shark may even be capable of surviving to 150, making it one of the longest-living creatures on earth.

MINI MONSTER
One of the smallest species of shark is the dwarf lantern that grows to about 20 cm (8 in) long.

WHOPPING WHALE
The largest species of shark (and the largest fish that has ever lived) is the whale shark. Exaggerated measurements of up to 18 m (60 ft) long and weighing 40 tonnes have been reported. Like great whales, these giants feed on plankton, which is how they got their name.

ENORMOUS EGGS
Scientists once thought that whale sharks laid huge eggs 30 cm (12 in) long, but they give birth to live young.

GROWING PAINS
The fastest developers are large pelagic sharks, such as blue sharks; they can grow up to 30 cm (12 in) in a single year.

PLENTIFUL FOOD
Possibly the most common shark throughout the world is the spiny (piked) dogfish, which is also eaten more widely than any other type. Because of this, its numbers are declining significantly.

DANGER!
Amanzimtoti beach in South Africa is one of the most dangerous beaches in the world for shark attacks.

ANCIENT SURVIVOR
The frilled shark resembles primitive extinct sharks in that it has six pairs of gill slits.

Gill slit

YAWNING HOLE
The jaws of *Carcharocles megalodon*, ancient ancestor of the great white shark, were 6 ft 6 in (1.8 m) across; in contrast, those of the largest recorded great white measure only 23 in (58 cm). Megalodon's teeth were also twice as big as the great white's.

BAD GUYS
Great white sharks are responsible for more attacks on people than any other species of shark, but tiger, bull, and hammerhead sharks have also been known to attack humans.

Frilled shark

SHARK MANIA
Peter Benchley's novel *Jaws* is one of the world's best-selling fiction books, and the first film based on it is one of the top-grossing movies of all time.

PRIZE CATCH
Many records for the great white shark are exaggerated, such as the one caught near Malta in 1992, allegedly 24 ft (7.10 m) long and over 7,700 lbs (3,500 kg).

Find out more

Aquariums in many large cities, such as New York, Chicago, San Diego, Waikiki, London, and Sydney, have impressive shark displays, and most can provide comprehensive background information in the form of books and leaflets, photographs, lectures, and websites. Conservation organizations, such as the Shark Research Institute, also provide information about sharks and encourage young people to get involved. There are also programs where people can adopt a shark and find out about its progress.

The best way to learn about sharks is to see them in the wild. Sharks live in all oceans of the world but only a few kinds are found in polar waters. You can see some sharks from boats including basking sharks and even great white sharks. Learning how to snorkel and scuba dive will also give many opportunities to see sharks, such as reef sharks that live in tropical waters. Check first that any boat tour or dive trip to see sharks meets with conservation guidelines.

BEHIND BARS
Those who want to study, photograph, or just observe sharks at close range usually do so from the safety of a strong metal cage. In ordinary circumstances, these cages have several attached floats, so the occupants are never more than about 10 ft (3 m) below the surface of the water.

Shark cages are designed for protection against larger sharks—smaller species can slip through the gaps.

An angel shark's eyes are on top of its head.

LOOKING SHARP
People from many cultures have made jewelry from sharks' teeth, sometimes in the hope that it would make the wearer as strong and frightening as the shark. This necklace of great white teeth comes from New Zealand. Natural history or anthropology museums often display similar objects.

VISIONS OF ANGELS
Angel sharks are a popular aquarium attraction; specimens are sometimes difficult to spot, however, since their mottled skin provides perfect camouflage against the sand and rocks on the bottom.

Places to visit

WAIKIKI AQUARIUM, WAIKIKI, HAWAII
Focusing on the aquatic life of the Pacific Ocean around Hawaii, this attraction includes more than 2,500 organisms representing over 420 species of animal and plant. Shark enthusiasts can view the Shark Cam, which keeps constant watch on the Hunters on the Reef exhibit so the habits and behavior of the creatures (rays, snappers, jacks, and groupers as well as sharks) can be studied closely.

NATURAL HISTORY MUSEUM OF LOS ANGELES, LOS ANGELES CALIFORNIA
A world leader in the field of natural history, this museum contains more than 33 million specimens and related artifacts. Shark buffs will not want to miss the rare megamouth shark, the first of its species to be exhibited in a museum and only the 11th to be found since its discovery in 1976.

NATIONAL AQUARIUM BALTIMORE, MARYLAND
A darkened shark exhibit allows close inspection of large sharks such as sand tiger and nurse sharks. The Wings in the Water exhibit lets visitors watch zebra sharks swim extremely close to the divers who feed them.

SHEDD AQUARIUM, CHICAGO, ILLINOIS
One of the world's largest displays of aquatic life, Shedd Aquarium provides an up-close experience with sharks, including blacktip reef sharks, zebra sharks, and sandbar sharks. Visitors are inches away from more than 30 sharks in a curved, overhead 400,000-gallon (1.5 million-liter) tank.

AQUARIUM OF THE AMERICAS NEW ORLEANS, LOUISIANA
Pet a baby shark in the Touch Pool and see one of the most diverse shark collections in the United States, including species rarely found in aquariums.

SEA WORLD, ORLANDO, FLORIDA
Sharks, eels, and barracuda make this underwater world their home. Visitors can travel through the world's largest underwater acrylic tunnel to get a close look at these dangerous creatures of the sea.

NEW YORK AQUARIUM, BROOKLYN, NEW YORK
The aquarium offers a look at more than 8,000 animals that include jellyfish in the new Alien Stingers exhibit, Walruses in the Sea Cliffs exhibit, and sea lions in an Aquatheater presentation.

SEA WORLD, SAN ANTONIO, TEXAS
Touch and feed bottle-nosed dolphins, see animal shows, and go on water rides at the world's largest marine life adventure park. There is another Sea World in San Diego, California.

SHARK ENCOUNTER
A clear observation tunnel at the Sydney Aquarium allows visitors to feel as if they are strolling along the ocean floor among the creatures that live there. Many aquariums exhibit some large sharks such as sand tigers and nurse sharks. Even whale sharks are on show in Japan and Atlanta, Georgia, and young great whites in Monterey, California.

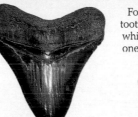

Fossil megalodon tooth (left) and great white tooth (below) one-quarter of their real sizes.

USEFUL WEBSITES

- Official Web site of the Shark Research Institute, a leading nonprofit, international organization concerned with conservation:
  www.sharks.org
- The International Shark Attack File with information and statistics on shark attacks worldwide:
  www.flmnh.ufl.edu/fish
- Official Web site of the Shedd Aquarium:
  www.sheddnet.org
- The National Aquarium in Baltimore has information on many different species of shark:
  www.aqua.org
- Learn shark terms using the Shark School's glossary:
  www.sdnhm.org/kids/sharks
- Test your knowledge with National Geographic's Shark Surfari online quiz:
  www.nationalgeographic.com/sharks
- See shark pictures, learn shark facts, and download shark activites on a kid-friendly Web site:
  www.kidzone.ws/sharks
- Get answers to questions on a variety of topics, from shark intelligence to shark attacks:
  www.sharkfoundation.com/facts.htm

Leopard shark

Early coconut-shell rattle for attracting sharks, from Samoa in the South Pacific

Glossary

ADAPTATION Evolutionary biological process that enables a species to adjust to its environment.

AMPULLAE OF LORENZINI Sensory pores on a shark's snout connected to delicate, jelly-filled internal canals; they are able to detect electric pulses from potential prey as it passes through the water. Scientists believe the ampullae of Lorenzini may also be involved in migration, acting as a kind of natural compass.

ANAL FIN One of the fins located on the underside of the body in some sharks.

Barbel

Nurse shark

BARBEL Fleshy, sensitive projection on the front of the mouth in certain species. Barbels probe mud or sand on the seabed to detect hidden food, and they may also help the shark to smell and taste.

CARTILAGE Firm, gristly tissue that forms the skeleton of sharks. While cartilage is flexible, it is not as hard as bone.

CARTILAGINOUS In describing an animal species, cartilaginous means having a skeleton made of cartilage rather than bone. Cartilaginous fish include sharks, skates, rays, and chimeras. (*see also* CARTILAGE)

CAUDAL FIN Tail fin. Within the various species, sharks have caudal fins of many different shapes and sizes.

CHUM Special shark bait consisting of blood mixed with salty, rotting fish.

CLASPERS Reproductive organs on the inner edge of a male shark's pelvic fins, through which sperm is released.

CLOACA Reproductive and excretory opening in the body of a fish.

COMMENSAL Relating to a connection between two organisms in which one benefits and the other is neither helped nor harmed. Pilot fish and sharks, for example, have a commensal relationship: pilot fish gain protection by swimming underneath sharks, which are not affected by this in any way.

COPEPOD One of more than 4,500 species of tiny aquatic animals that are a major component of plankton. Some of these attach themselves to sharks' fins and gills, feeding off skin secretions and blood.

CORNEA Tough but transparent membrane that covers the iris and pupil in the eyes of vertebrates, octopuses, and squids.

CRUSTACEA One of a group of hard-shelled aquatic creatures such as crab and shrimp that provide food for some types of shark.

DENTINE Dense material made from minerals that forms the principal component of teeth.

DERMAL DENTICLES Literally, "skin teeth," which act like scales to form a protective coat of armor on a shark's body. Similar to conventional teeth, these are made up of dentine and enamel, but they are shaped differently according to where they appear: the ones on the snout are rounded, while those on the back are pointed. Dermal denticles are ridged, and they line up with the direction the shark is moving to minimize drag. (*see also* DENTINE)

DORSAL Relating to an animal's back (opposite of VENTRAL).

Dorsal fin

Caudal (tail) fin

Dogfish embryo

DORSAL FIN One of the fins located on the midline of a fish's back to stop it from rolling from side to side.

ECHINODERM One of a group of marine invertebrates that provide food for some types of shark.

ECOLOGY The study of how organisms relate to each other and their environment. Experts who specialize in this field are called ecologists.

ECOSYSTEM Collection of interacting organisms within a particular habitat.

ENAMEL Outer coating of teeth. Enamel is the hardest substance in an animal's body.

EMBRYO Developing animal before it is born or hatched from an egg.

FEEDING FRENZY The uncontrolled behavior of a group of sharks when there is blood or food in the water. During a feeding frenzy, sharks are not concerned for their own safety, and may even attack one another.

FOSSIL Remains of ancient plant or animal that have been preserved in soil or rock.

Dermal denticles

GALL BLADDER Small pouch that stores bile, which is produced by the liver to aid in digestion.

GESTATION The period, between conception and birth, in which an embryo develops.

GILL RAKER Comblike organ on the gill arch of some sharks. Its function is to strain plankton out of water taken into the shark's mouth.

Black tip reef shark

A predatory bull shark hunting in the shallows.

OTOLITHS Calcium carbonate granules in a shark's ear that allow it to establish its angle of tilt in the water.

OPERCULUM Gill cover present in bony fish but not in sharks.

OMNIVOROUS Feeding on all types of food, both plant and animal.

OOPHAGY A form of prenatal cannibalism in which some developing sharks feed on eggs produced by the mother.

OLFACTORY Relating to a creature's sense of smell.

NICTITATING MEMBRANE Third, inner eyelid that moves across the surface of a shark's eye to clean and protect it. This function is similar to that of human eyelids when we blink.

MIGRATION Regular movement of an animal population from one area to another and back again, often on a yearly basis.

LATERAL LINE Row of pressure-sensitive organs that run along each side of a shark's body and around its head. These organs can alert the shark to the movement and the proximity of objects in the water by detecting tiny changes in pressure—a great advantage when the sea is dark or murky.

LAMELLAE Microscopic, capillary-filled branches that make up the feathery filaments lying across a fish's gill arches. These structures absorb oxygen and expel carbon dioxide.

Nurse-shark gills

INVERTEBRATE Animal without a backbone or spinal column (opposite of VERTEBRATE).

GILLS Breathing organs of fish through which oxygen is taken in and carbon dioxide is expelled. In sharks and closely related species, the gills appear as a series of between five and seven slits behind the head.

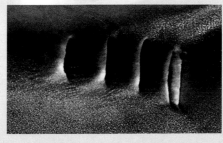

Tagging

VIVIPAROUS Producing young that remain in the mother's body until they are fully formed and ready to be born.

VERTICAL MIGRATION Movement of marine creatures from deep to shallow water or vice versa. Planktonic organisms migrate in this way daily, and they are often followed by fish, whales, and other, similar, predators.

VERTEBRATE Animal that has a backbone or spinal column (opposite of INVERTEBRATE).

VENTRAL Relating to the underside of the body (opposite of DORSAL).

TAPETUM Layer of cells lying behind the retina in the eyes of some fish and nocturnal animals. These cells reflect light, helping the creature to see in the dark.

TAGGING Method of tracking and studying sharks in the wild by attaching tags to their fins so their movements can be recorded.

SPIRAL VALVE Shark's efficient, corkscrew-shaped intestine.

SPIRACLE Additional, rounded gill opening on top of the head in some bottom-dwelling sharks.

SHAGREEN Dried shark skin used like sandpaper to polish wood and stone.

PREDATOR A creature whose natural inclination is to prey on other animals.

PLANKTON Microscopic, sometimes moving, organisms that provide food for some shark species. Whale sharks, for example, live mostly on plankton.

PELVIC FIN One of a pair of fins located on the underside of the rear section of a fish's body. Smaller than pectoral fins, pelvic fins also assist steering and act as stabilizers.

Horn shark

Pectoral fin

PECTORAL FIN One of a pair of fins located on the underside of the front section of a fish's body. Pectoral fins provide lift, assist steering, and act as brakes when necessary.

PARASITE Animal or plant that lives on another organism and draws nutrients from it.

OVOVIVIPAROUS Producing eggs that hatch inside the mother's body.

OVIPAROUS Producing eggs that hatch outside the mother's body.

OVIDUCT Egg tube of a female shark into which sperm is introduced by the male.

Index

Acknowledgments

Dorling Kindersley would like to thank: Alan Hills, John Williams, & Mike Row of the British Museum, Harry Taylor & Tim Parmenter of the Natural History Museum, Michael Dent, & Michael Pitts (Hong Kong) for additional special photography; the staff of Sea Life Centres (UK), especially Robin James & Ed Speight (Weymouth) & Rod Haynes (Blackpool), David Bird (Poole Aquarium), & Ocean Park Aquarium (Hong Kong), for providing specimens for photography & species information; the staff of the British Museum, Museum of Mankind, the Natural History Museum, especially Oliver Crimmen of the Fish Dept, the Marine Biological Association (UK), the Marine Conservation Society (UK), Sarah Powler of the Nature Conservation Bureau (UK), the Sydney Aquarium (Darling Harbour, Australia), John West of the Aust. Shark Attack File (Taronga Zoo, Australia), George Burgess of the International Shark Attack File (Florida Museum of Natural History, USA), Dr Peter Klimley (University of California, USA), & Rolf Williams for their research help; Djutja Djutja Munuygurr, Djapu artist, 1983/1984, tor bark painting; John Reynolds & the *Ganesha* (Cornwall) for the tagging sequence; Oliver Denton & Carly Nicolls as photographic models; Peter Bailey, Katie Davis (Australia), Muffy Dodson (Hong Kong), Chris Howson, Earl Neish, Manisha Patel, & Helena Spiteri for their design & editorial assistance; Jane Parker for the index; Julie Ferris for proofreading; & Margaret Parrish for Americanization.

Maps: Sallie Alane Reason.
Illustrations: John Woodcock .

Clip art: David Ekholm-JAlbum, Claire Ellerton, Sunita Gahir, Susan St. Louis, Lisa Stock, & Bulent Yusuf.
Wall chart: Neville Graham, Sue Nicholson, & Susan St. Louis.

Picture credits: a=above t=top b=bottom/below c=center l=left r= right

Ardea: Mark Heiches 52bl; D Parer & E Parer-Cook 19tc; Peter Sleyn 8b, 30bc; Ron & Val Taylor 7br, 38bl, 40cl, 41tr, 49ct, 52t, 52bc, 53tr, 53cr; Valerie Taylor 19bl, 31, 51c, 51bl, 60tr; Wardene Weisser 8c.
Aviation Picture Library / Austin J Brown: 35br. **BBC Natural History Unit:** Michael Pitts 64ca; Jeff Rotman 65tr, 66cla, 66bc, 67cla, 69c. **The British Museum/Museum of Mankind:** 46tl, 68bl, 69br. **Bridgeman:** The Prado (Madrid), *The Tooth Extractor* by Theodor Rombouts (1597–1637), 32bl; Private Collection, *The Little Mermaid* by E S Hardy, 21tl. **Corbis:** Will Burgess/Reuters 50cla; Paul A Souders 68–69. **Capricorn Press Pty:** 56tl, 56tr. **J Allan Cash:** 27br, 50tr, 51tlb. **Bruce Coleman Ltd:** 59c. **Neville Coleman Underwater Geographic Photo Agency:** 20cr, 44bl, 61cr. **Ben Cropp (Australia):** 50b.
C M Dixon: 47cr. **Dorling Kindersley:** Colin Keates 25tr, 32br; Kim Taylor 21tl; Jerry Young, 9cr, 42cr. **Richard Ellis** (USA): 17r. **Eric Le Feuvre** (USA): 20br.
Eric & David Hoskings: 56cl. **Frank Lane Picture Agency:** 30br. **Perry Gilbert** (USA): 51tr, 51trb. **Peter Goadby** (Australia): 28t. **Greenpeace:** 58tr; 59br. **T Britt Griswold:** 44b. **Tom Haight** (USA): 45t. **Sonia Halliday &**

Laura Lushington: 50tl. **Robert Harding Picture Library:** 18tr. Edward S Hodgson (USA): 60lb, 61lb. **The Hulton Picture Company:** 34tl, 42cl. **Hunterian Museum, The University of Glasgow:** 13c. **The Image Bank /** Guido Alberto Rossi: 30t. **Intervideo Television Clip Entertainment Group Ltd:** 6t. F Jack Jackson: 49cr, 49br. **Grant Johnson:** 54clb. C Scott Johnson (USA): 50cb. Stephane Korb (France): 58cr, 58b. **William MacQuitty International Collection:** 48bc. **Mary Evans Picture Library:** 10t, 36t, 38t, 40t, 48tl, 52tl, 55br, 60tl. **National Museum of Natural History, Smithsonian Institution** (Washington, DC): Photo Chip Clark 13r. **NHPA:** Joe B Blossom 23cr; John Shaw 23tl; ANT/Kelvin Aitken 48cr. **National Marine Fisheries Service:** H Wes Pratt 54ct, 59tl; Greg Skomal 54bl; Charles Stillwell 23tc, 23tr. **Ocean Images:** Rosemary Chastney 28b, 29b, 29c, 54cl; Walt Clayton 15br, 49cl; Al Giddings 15cr, 45br, 48cl, 49bl, 53bl; Charles Nicklin 29br; Doc White 20cl, 20bcl. **Oceanwide Images:** Gary Bell 54cla. **Oxford Scientific Films:** Fred Bavendam 25cl, 39b; Tony Crabtree 34b, 35t; Jack Dermid 25cr; Max Gibbs 27cbr; Rudie Kuiter 431; Godfrey Merlen 43br; Peter Porks 35c; Kirn Westerskov, 49tr; Norbert Wu 45cr. **Planet Earth Pictures:** Richard Cook 59bl; Walter Deas 24bc, 39c, 48bl; Daniel W Gotsholl 30cl; Jack Johnson 51br; A Kerstitch 21cr, 21bc, 21b; Ken Lucas 20tr, 24cr, 39tr, 42bl; Krov Menhuin 27bl; D Murrel 32t; Doug Perrine, 23br, 25t, 26bcr, 54br, 55tr, 55br; Christian Petron 42br; Brian Pitkin 24tl; Flip Schulke 30tl; Marty Snyderman 20bl, 27t, 42t, 43t, 54cr; James P Watt 32t, 32b, 33t, 33b; Marc Webber 30bl; Norbert Wu 26c, 48br. **Courtesy of**

Sea Life Centres (UK): 62bl. **Shark Angling Club of Great Britain:** 58cl. **The Shark Trust:** 63tr. Courtesy of Sydney Aquarium (Darling Harbour, Australia): 62br. **Werner Forman Archive /** Museum of Mankind: 47cl. **Courtesy of Wilkinson Sword:** 60cl. Rolf Williams: 16tl, 18cr (in block of six), 59tr, 61tr.

Wall chart credits: Ardea: Valerie Taylor cra (hammerhead); **DK Images:** Natural History Museum, London cb (gill rakers), cb (jaw), cb (teeth); **Getty Images:** Jeffrey L. Rotman / Photonica cla (danger sign); Photographer's Choice / Georgette Douwma cb (turtle); **Photoshot / NHPA:** A.N.T. Photo Library cb (whale shark) **Marty Snyderman Productions:** clb.

Jacket credits: *Front:* **DK Images:** British Museum tr; **Imagestate:** First Light c; **OSF:** Max Gibbs tl. *Back:* **DK Images:** British Museum bc, ca, cb, clb, Natural History Museum, London crb.

All other images © Dorling Kindersley. For further information see: www.dkimages.com